An Emotional Devotional

By

Sherry Pierce

Note for Librarians: a cataloguing record for this book that includes Dewey Decimal Classification and US Library of Congress numbers is available from the Library and Archives of Canada. The complete cataloguing record can be obtained from their online database at:
www.collectionscanada.ca/amicus/index-e.html
ISBN 1-4120-3852-9
Printed in Victoria, BC, Canada

TRAFFORD

Offices in Canada, USA, Ireland, UK and Spain
This book was published *on-demand* in cooperation with Trafford Publishing. On-demand publishing is a unique process and service of making a book available for retail sale to the public taking advantage of on-demand manufacturing and Internet marketing. On-demand publishing includes promotions, retail sales, manufacturing, order fulfilment, accounting and collecting royalties on behalf of the author.
Book sales for North America and international:
Trafford Publishing, 6E–2333 Government St.,
Victoria, BC v8t 4p4 CANADA
phone 250 383 6864 (toll-free 1 888 232 4444)
fax 250 383 6804; email to orders@trafford.com
Book sales in Europe:
Trafford Publishing (uk) Ltd., Enterprise House, Wistaston Road Business Centre, Wistaston Road, Crewe, Cheshire cw2 7rp UNITED KINGDOM
phone 01270 251 396 (local rate 0845 230 9601)
facsimile 01270 254 983; orders.uk@trafford.com
Order online at:
www.trafford.com/robots/04-1660.html

10 9 8 7 6 5 4 3

Table of Contents

Acknowledgements

I must first thank my Lord and Savior Jesus Christ for His incredible grace and gift of salvation, without which I would be lost! And for the inspiration to write this book to encourage others along the way!

I praise God for...

My wonderful husband Larry, what a gift you are to me. I can't imagine life without you. You keep me laughing and I love you dearly!

My awesome children and their families, I love you with all my heart; you have blessed me in more ways than you realize and I consider it a privilege to be your mother and friend.

My parents and sisters, you have helped make me the "crazy character" I am, and taught me very valuable life lessons. I love you.

My Auntie Mimi, you have prayed for me without ceasing since I was knee-high to a grasshopper and I am forever grateful!

My incredible friends, brothers and sisters in the Lord, who shall remain nameless as I would never want to hurt any of you by naming some and forgetting others, we've laughed, cried, and prayed together, encouraged each other, held each other accountable, and sharpened each other as iron. I truly am rich in friends, thank you for laughing at my jokes, even when they weren't funny! You're great and I love you all.

Ray Comfort, Kirk Cameron, Darrel Rundus, Living Waters and The Way of the Master Team; your perseverance and unwavering dedication to seek and save the lost, and to see people soundly saved, has sparked a fire in me to do the same. I have been forever changed by your ministry and friendship.

Jan Ayers, whose heart art, captured a beautiful picture, of the masterpiece God has made out of all of these emotions. I am thrilled and honored to have it on the cover of this book. What an incredible gift!

Last but not least, Deborah Shambora, for using your God-given talent in designing the cover of this book, formatting it so it's readable, and your numerous other selfless acts along the way.
To my "Russian Roomy" and friend, may God richly bless you for all you have done!

"What Lenses are You Looking Through?"

My husband was blessed with excellent eyesight. At least until he turned 40. At that age, he started needing reading glasses, and as the years have progressed, it's gotten worse. He has now graduated to progressive tri-focals.

I, on the other hand, have worn glasses since the 4th grade. I lived through, and heard, every four-eyes joke there is. I've had an array of stylish glasses. The most memorable were the tortoise shell, kidney bean shaped glasses, as well as the wire rimmed, stop sign shaped beauties. Of course, I had to have the huge red glasses like the talk show host, Sally Jesse Raphael. She looked so adorable in them. It wasn't until years later, after developing some old film that I discovered I looked anything but adorable! Some things really should, be left to the professionals.

Thankfully, contacts were invented, and I have been wearing them ever since. My husband has always gotten a good laugh whenever I would remove my contacts before establishing where my glasses were first! I would feel my way around the room, patting everything in sight in desperate search of my glasses. Oh yes, this was great entertainment for him, that is, until his eyes started failing. Now, my entertainment has begun.

One day, my husband was complaining of a canker sore he had, and he went upstairs to put some medicine on it to help alleviate the pain. Canker sores are so small, but they can be so painful, and this one was on his tongue. Ouch!

Within minutes, I heard a yell, and then here he came running down the stairs tongue hanging out and a bottle of medicine in hand, demanding, " HONEY, WHA, ITH, THITH?"

What?

He grew more desperate, " WHA ITH THITH?"

I looked, and there in his hand, he held the bottle of "Freezone" corn and callous remover. He was not wearing his glasses and had applied this to his tongue, mistaking it for the canker sore medicine. He said it felt like it was on fire, and now I could see that his tongue was white, and hard as a rock. At least we were assured that no corn would grow there in the near future.

I'm afraid I must be honest and tell you that, I broke out in hysterical laughter and it was clear that my husband did not find this funny. I thought I would die from laughing, but quickly realized that I must compose myself. This was poison he had just ingested, and I needed to call the Poison Control Center. So with all the strength I could muster, I placed the call. I am proud to say that I calmly explained the situation to the representative. Freezone corn and callous remover had accidentally been applied to a canker sore on the tongue. The center had never heard of this happening, so after a quick check the representative returned to the line with specific instructions. Do not throw up. Drink plenty of milk to help counteract the poison. And, by no means should he try to pick this off of his tongue or it would tear off part of his tongue. It needed to wear itself off gradually.

She asked what his name was and I replied, "Larry." Then, it happened!

She asked, "How old is little Larry?" That's it! I could hold it no longer. I busted out in a rolling heap as I declared, "48!" Then she joined in on this laughter and it was all over. We had lost control. Poor Larry just stood there, tongue hanging out, as we continued on at his expense.

The next day, someone from Poison Control called to check on "little Larry" and it started all over again. Through the years, Larry and I have had many a belly laugh over this. Well, I guess I've had many belly laughs. His are more like a slight chuckle. Don't worry, his tongue healed just fine and his canker sore was gone! Needless to say, when applying anything now, "little Larry" makes sure he has on his glasses.

This got me thinking. How many times have we looked at things through our own eyes, only to later learn that we have been deceived by something that appeared right, and we wound up getting hurt. Our eyes can deceive us, but God never will. God cannot lie! When we look at things through the lenses of the Lord, and keep our eyes fixed on Jesus, our vision is clear and our path is sure. He makes no mistakes. Oh, that we would always view things the way God sees them.

Father, Unveil my eyes, that I might see all You have in store for me. Open the eyes of my heart, so that I can see clearly, from the start, Your view of others, and how I should be from now until eternity. In Jesus' name, AMEN.

7

Are You a "Real" Fisherman?

My husband loves to fish, and I like to fish. Our styles are different however.

First, I must give you a little history. When I met my husband, he was tournament bass fishing, almost every weekend. He had a bass boat that would reach speeds of 73 mph, in order to get to the "fish" first! He had every kind of tackle you can imagine. Plastic worms, spinner bait, crank bait, top water bait. I still don't know what they all are. There was even special goo to squirt on the plastic worms so that they smelled real. I never understood why he didn't just use a real worm; it seemed much easier. He had an electric fish finder showing where the fish were in the water and how deep they were. And if that wasn't enough, there was a graph that charted out the topography of the bottom of the lake and printed out onto paper where the fish were in relation to it.

My husband will fish in the bitter cold at the crack of

dawn with icicles forming on the fishing line, or in the heat of the summer in sweltering temperatures with the sun beating down and no shade for hours. He is serious about his fishing, and he is good at it. He doesn't eat until fish are caught, and he doesn't like anything that disturbs the fishing process.

I did not know his style when I decided to go fishing with him. I was looking forward to it. I have memories as a child standing in the water catching blue gill on a stick, one right after another. It was so much fun! Since this wasn't a tournament, I thought it would be fun to fish together.

I also enjoy camping, so I thought we could sleep until 8am and then I'd cook us a nice breakfast before fishing at 10. You can imagine my surprise when I was awakened at dawn to begin our adventure. Hungry and tired, I stumbled around preparing everything I would need for the day. No time to shave my legs-no problem-we'll be in the water, I can do that on the boat. I packed some snacks and some sodas, grabbed my book and away we went.

As we shot across the water at breakneck speeds, I struggled to open my eyes to see who we were racing to "the spot". Risking my contacts blowing off my eyeballs, I squinted and looked around, anxious to see if we were in the lead. We were! No one else was even on the lake! We arrived at our destination, and my husband quickly cast out with one of the 17 fishing poles he needs, each one with a different lure, so as not to waste time changing them. As I debated as to what lure I would use, I looked through his tackle box and chose a beautiful purple worm. He patiently explained to me that the fish were not biting the purple worm this time of year, and that I should use the chartreuse one. The chartreuse one? It's not nearly as pretty as the purple. Besides they're fish-do they really care which color? I mean if they are dumb enough to bite a plastic worm, why would they be picky about color? So I ignored his advice and cast out the pretty purple worm, only

to discover that he was right-no bites on that one. So I reluc-
tantly tied on the chartreuse one, and cast out. I was expecting
immediate results. After all, I was now using the color of
choice for them. After a few casts, my patience had worn thin
with this "fake bait". I decided to break out the good stuff.
Night crawlers! After gently explaining to the little worm how
sorry I was about sticking him, I cast him out into the deep
blue yonder. I sat down, got out my book, and started to read
with one hand while holding my pole with the other. After
awhile, I found myself getting sleepy, and I was afraid my pole
might fall into the water if I nodded off, so I decided this
would be a good time to shave my legs-that'll wake me up.

I whipped out the shaving cream, spread it on, and
flung my leg over the side of the boat and began shaving. I
thought my husband was going to have a coronary. He was
hollering something about how the fish will never bite now
and, what was I doing blah, blah, blah. I couldn't see what the
big fuss was all about. You mean to tell me that these brilliant
fish that bite plastic worms are going to be turned off by a little shaving cream? Give me a break. I finished my shaving and
cast out again. Now I was getting hungry, so I decided it was
time for a snack. After all, we hadn't had breakfast. He just
stared at me in disbelief as I crunched my Fritos, drank my
soda, read my book, and balanced my pole between my knees.

Meanwhile, he kept diligently casting off the front of
the boat. I was engrossed in my novel, when a bee started
swarming around my head. I took my pole and, while keeping
my bait in the water, started to swat at it. All of a sudden there
was a tug on the line and before you know it, I had reeled in a
nice bass. I put on another night crawler, apologizing again,
and cast out. Soon here came that stupid bee again. I began
swatting and it happened again, another nice fish. Now, I had
my husband's attention! He came to the back of the boat and
began fishing beside me. But, he still had the rubber worm, I
had the real one. Soon, I caught another. This was more than

10

he could take and before long, he was begging to use one of my night crawlers. He sat very low in the boat to tie it on, so as not to be seen by any other fishermen going by. He was afraid they might see him and word would get out that he had sold out to using regular worms. He began moving his pole around as if swatting a bee and soon he was catching them too!

I've thought about our fishing experiences with a smile quite often. My husband really is a good fisherman, and he has taught me a lot. Things like where to cast, and when to cast, how deep, and what kind of lure to use depending upon the conditions. These things are all important. We learned that day though, that when you have the "real" stuff, it makes all the difference in your catching ability.

Jesus said, "Follow me and I will make you fishers of men." Fishing for people is a lot like fishing for fish. You need to have the "real bait". Your life is a testimony. If your relationship with Jesus is not real, it will show. You must know where to cast and when to cast. You need to pray and ask the Holy Spirit to go before you and prepare the way, so the conditions will be right. We need to be serious about fishing. We must not fish in fear that someone may notice we are talking about Jesus. We'll never catch one that way.

Jesus said in Mark 8:38, "For whoever is ashamed of Me and My words in this adulterous and sinful generation, the Son of Man will also be ashamed of him when He comes in glory of His Father with the holy angels."

Lord, help me to be a fisher of men. Give me wisdom and discernment of timing in sharing the good news of Your grace with those I come in contact with today. Soften their hearts, and bring clarity to my lips, that I may speak Your truth, and that truth set them free. Make me bold and confident in You, not ashamed to proclaim that You are the Way, the Truth, and the Life, and that no one comes to the Father except through You.
In Jesus' name, Amen.

11

"Confessions of a Church Nazi"

When I asked Jesus to be my Savior, I was overwhelmed with the knowledge of my sin against a Holy God. I was so deeply sorry, and I just wanted every piece of filth in my life gone! I knew that, since I had asked for forgiveness, Jesus had cleansed me from all unrighteousness. Now I wanted everything around me cleansed as well-hence came the reign of 'The Church Nazi!' At least, that's what my children called me.

Church attendance was not an option, all must attend. Now this could be maddening at times for a church Nazi because maintaining control was difficult. While I would be singing on the praise team, praising the Lord, I would look out over the congregation only to see my teenagers making faces and mimicking me while I was singing. Please tell me, how was a woman to worship?

At home, however, Biblical Boot camp was in full force,

complete with music, movie, and book inspections.

Everyone was made aware of the rules. Anything inappropriate was thrown out or destroyed, and replaced with something more suitable. All new purchases had to meet the requirements: no foul language or lewd behavior advocated; must meet parental approval. Anything not meeting the guidelines would be promptly returned to the store! There were periodic searches, with confiscation of smuggled in material. Oh yes, I said smuggled! Our teenagers knew the rules, and yet they would still try to hide it, in hopes I wouldn't notice. But, the church Nazi was sharp on her toes. I would destroy it, and wait for them to ask where it was. I will admit my husband and I would giggle, watching them try to discreetly run around and figure out what happened to their prized possession. On occasion, they grew brave and would ask, citing that the music was not theirs, but a friend had lent it. That was fine-the friend just needed to ask me for it back-no problem! That never happened and soon the lending stopped also.

Now, there were still some areas of the house that had never occurred to me to clean out. For instance, I had forgotten that we had a cabinet in the garage full of liqueur. These were bottles my husband had collected for years, expensive gifts from business associates, never opened, still in their little velvet bags, collecting dust. One day, while in the kitchen cleaning out the refrigerator, I heard this; "Throw out all of the alcohol now." What? "THROW OUT ALL OF THE ALCOHOL---NOW!" I just knew this was the voice of the Lord, after all I had completely forgotten about the alcohol. I immediately went to the garage and gathered all the bottles. I began dumping them down the drain-oh the stench! The house smelled like a brewery! I then threw all the bottles in the garbage can outside. It filled that big can halfway full. I have always wondered what the garbage men thought of that. I didn't tell my husband, because I didn't know how I was going to explain to him that I heard the Lord tell me to do this. At that time in his life, he

13

wouldn't have understood. He was out of town anyway, and I just hoped he didn't notice, and he never did.

Months later, during a discussion with our daughters, they asked, "Mom, how do you know everything we do? Who has been telling you?" I told them that I pray and ask God for wisdom as to how to raise them, and to please show me what to do, and He does. They didn't believe me, so I began to explain the alcohol example. One of our daughters, along with my husband, became white as a sheet, but for different reasons. I apologized to my husband for not telling him sooner. I explained that I had sensed such an urgency that I had to follow through with what the Lord was telling me. Before he could say anything, our daughter began to share that she had discovered the alcohol when she was at home alone one day. She drank some of it, and couldn't wait to tell her sisters about her amazing find. They all jumped in on the story at this point and began to tell about how the very next day she told them about the alcohol, but said that they would have to find it. So they played the "hot and cold" game. They would look all over while she would say, you're getting colder, or warmer etc. until they discovered it. When they opened the cabinet where it had been-it was empty!!!! The girls never believed that she had found anything, and she was terrified after that.

To God be the glory!

I thank God, and I know that He saved our family from the destruction the enemy had planned.

2nd Timothy 2:21-22 says; "Therefore if anyone cleanses himself from these things, he will be a vessel for honor, sanctified, useful to the Master, prepared for every good work. Now flee from youthful lusts and pursue righteousness, faith, love and peace, with those who call on the Lord from a pure heart." In this day and time, there is so much immorality, it is all around us. We must be vigilant, in our desire to abstain from all ungodliness.

Romans 12:2 says; And do not be conformed to this world, but be transformed by the renewing of your mind, so that you may prove what the will of God is, that which is good an acceptable and perfect.

We must put on the Lord Jesus Christ, not just believe in Him!

Oh Lord,

It is our desire to be a living and holy sacrifice, acceptable to You. Help us not to be conformed to this world. Cleanse us from all immorality, and renew our minds, so that we will know Your perfect will. Strengthen us to walk the path You have laid before us as we seek to honor You. In Jesus' name, Amen.

No More Infomercials

It's a known fact in our household that my husband and I cannot watch infomercials. My husband loves to flip through the channels; of course I don't know a man who doesn't. Anyway, he sometimes stops at an infomercial, and the scenario is always the same. I say, "Honey, change the channel. You know we can't watch this. We don't need what they are selling."

But it isn't long before we are both sold, and soon I'm scrambling to write down the telephone number so we can call within the next 2 minutes to avoid losing all the added extras on this chance of a lifetime!

I do have to say that the beef jerky was awesome that I made in the food dehydrator, the two times I used it. Of course, the infrared oven's possibilities were endless, and warranted paying the extra shipping to get it here faster. I don't know how we had survived without it that long. Then, there was the diet plan we ordered, determined to take control of our weight. I did lose almost 30lbs, or was that from dusting all the exercise machines we had needed over the years? I know it wasn't from eating the healthy snacks I read about in the cookbook I ordered. Every time I read them they sound so delicious, but I have yet to actually have one touch my lips!

"Tae-bo" was finally the answer to me getting in shape. I methodically went through the motions, ignoring the pain pulsating through my body as I worked to achieve the "video body" I was watching. When I breathlessly answered the phone, my daughter became concerned that I was experiencing a heart attack. She demanded that I rest, and wanted to know what on earth I was doing. After I answered, "Tae-bo" she seemed to be impressed, that is, until I confessed that I was only in the instructional portion of the video and had not actually reached the full workout phase yet. Laughter could be heard for miles!

That was enough of that. Then I heard about "Spiritual Tae-bo". I had to have it. I just knew that it wouldn't painful, and I would be drawing closer to the Lord while exercising. Finally, the answer! Let me just tell you now, and save you some money-there is nothing spiritual about exercise! It still hurts, and you still get sore. I do remember thinking, "OH LORD, WHY AM I TRYING THIS AGAIN?" Does that count as spiritual?

"Pilates" was much less strenuous and may have worked, had it not been for the uncontrollable outburst of laughter spilling from my daughter while watching me attempt it. I'm not sure her stomach muscles could take the strain again. And, lest we forget about the infamous "Abdomenizer" guaranteed to flatten your stomach in 10 short days. Just hook it on the door like a huge slingshot, and enjoy exercising. One word of caution from my husband, LOCK THE DOOR before using, or someone like your wife, could innocently open the door and you'll experience more than just a flattened stomach!

Our latest purchase was bicycles for each other. They are wonderful. They shift themselves automatically for an easy smooth ride, with little or no strain.

Our daughter asked," What about when you want a workout?" .

To which I replied," Who wants a workout?" I'm through being her entertainment!

Wherever you go, it seems as though someone is always coming up with something better, the latest and greatest. When we get something we think we need that is missing from our life, we are soon dismayed to learn that there is soon something better. Funny how we don't realize we need Jesus when He is missing in our life. Nothing will ever be better than Him. He is definitely something we can't afford to be without, and you don't have to call within the next 2 minutes. In fact, our lives are actually in serious trouble without Him. When we chase the things of this world, we will pay dearly. Any day now, our life will be required of us, and we will be judged. And if we don't have Jesus, we are headed for hell. It's as simple as that. He offers us the gift of grace. We can't buy it. In fact, we can't even earn it. We must receive it by faith. All we have to do is repent, and ask Him for forgiveness from our sin and allow Him to lead our life from here on out. There is no greater offer than that!

The Bible says," For what does it profit a man to gain the whole world, and forfeit his soul?"(Mark 8:36) What things have we gained that couldn't be lost tomorrow?

In Matthew 6:19-21 it says," Do not store up for yourselves treasures on earth, where moth and rust destroy, and where thieves break in and steal. But store up for yourselves, treasures in heaven, where neither moth, nor rust destroy, and where thieves do not break

18

in or steal. For where your treasure is, there your heart will be also.

So let me ask you..."Where is your treasure? Where is your heart?" Maybe you've gotten caught up in the "stuff" of this world. We can have the latest and greatest, but if we don't have Jesus, we are LOST! Jesus needs to be number one in our life-above anyone or anything. And if He isn't, then our priorities are in the wrong place and we are in serious danger! Let's ask the Lord to prioritize our life today.

Dear Lord,

Thank you for letting me see clearly that the only thing I need is You. Forgive me for my selfish and sinful actions, and from this day forward, let all I do honor You. Help me to put You first, above all else in my life. Lead and direct me in each step I take, and each decision I make. I want to invest in things eternal - not of this world.

In Jesus' name, AMEN.

Frozen in Fear

Have you ever been to the Grand Canyon and viewed its majestic beauty? It's incredible to see the color of the canyon as the rays of sunlight bounce off the walls. You can't help but feel close to the Lord when you are overlooking this master-piece.

My husband was born and raised in Arizona and had never been to the Grand Canyon, so we decided to take a trip, just the two of us. We had a great time. While my husband fed the squirrels, I read a book to him about white water river rafting the canyon. We ate ice cream and walked together, noting the hikers that were headed down into the base of the canyon for what would be an extensive journey.

Eventually we boarded a bus to tour the area. The driver would stop at certain points and share interesting facts about the park. At different times he would offer the option of getting off the bus for a nearby hiking trail, for those who wished to see more. He'd give the distance of the trail and invite anyone to feel free to get back on the bus at the next stop. We toyed with the idea of hiking so when he announced the last opportunity, a one mile trail, we decided to go for it. One mile would be a drop in the bucket. We were already used to walking several miles each day for exercise anyway. As we walked along the trail, we marveled at the incredible beauty! You could hear the wind blow through the canyon and feel the breeze on your face. So quiet and serene, it seemed as though our whispers echoed back at us.

Gradually the trail began to narrow and as it did, it drew closer and closer to the edge. I am extremely fearful of heights. This I already knew, but I had no idea just how extreme that fear was. As I walked along, my steps grew slower and slower. My husband was leading the way, and he kept calling back to me to hurry up! As the trail grew thinner and closer to the edge of a sheer drop off, with nothing in between, the ability for me to move became less and less, until finally it stopped. I could go no further. I was frozen in fear and I don't even know if I was breathing at that point. I know I had to have been, but it was very shallow and limited.

My husband grew frustrated that I seemed to have ignored his request, and he headed back towards me to see what the problem was. When he saw the tears streaming down my face, and my inability to answer him or even move, his eyes grew soft with compassion. He realized I was terrified. He apologized and then offered to help me. Inch by inch we crept along with him holding my hand and assuring me it was going to be all right. Eventually he led me to the end, and we finished the trail. Our one mile hike had actually taken two hours. To this day, that memory is still etched in my mind. I remember the depth of love with which my husband gently walked me through that very frightening time.

What a beautiful picture of how God is with us. We are

walking along the path of life, having a great time taking in the scenery, when gradually circumstances close in on us and we find ourselves paralyzed by fear or hopelessness and can't seem to move. It's at those moments God holds our hand and inches us forward.

I look back now and think, why was I so scared? The worst thing that could have happened to me was falling to my death, and I'd be with Jesus, so how is that bad? Sometimes looking back on our circumstances, we question why we were fearful when we know God is in control.

Psalm 121: 1-3 says; I will lift up my eyes to the hills-from whence come my help? My help comes from the Lord, Who made heaven and earth. He will not allow your foot to be moved; He who keeps you will not slumber.

He also promises that He will never leave us nor forsake us, so remember the next time that you are frozen in fear, that the God of the universe, who made heaven and earth, is holding your hand and will never let go.

Lord,

Thank You for the love and mercy with which You have carried me through my weakest moments. You have carefully moved me forward when I thought I couldn't go on. In my life ahead, when I am troubled, remind me of Your faithfulness and that You will never leave me nor forsake me.
My trust is in You, Lord. I abide in the shadow of Your wing and I am hidden in the Cleft of the Rock, and there is no safer place to be. Thank You for loving me so.

In Jesus' name, AMEN

Grandmas are Great!

I'm in the hood---Grandparenthood! Yep, my grandchildren call me Grammy. Aren't grandchildren great? You can have so much fun with them. I love to spoil them-give them some chocolate and then send them home :.

And when it's time for gifts-well, I think every grandchild should have finger paints, don't you?

Hey, I paid my dues! I went through the FUN gifts with my children. The toys that made your check book look like the national debt because of battery purchases. Um hmm. Or how about the play dough that always seemed more attractive on the carpet! And, lest we forget, the wooden hammer that accompanies the cute little blocks that you are suppose to strike with it. Of course, my son struck everything but the blocks, including my head! Even the dog wasn't safe.

Oh yes-I have paid my dues-now it is my turn to have

fun, and I'm going to make the most of it:!

Grandmas are wonderful. Are any of you a grandma, or still have a grandma? Grandmas have a way of always seeing the good in you. And they have time to play! Now, I'm not proud of this fact, but it seems as parents, we can be so busy at times. I remember one day one of my daughters saying, "Mommy, can you please play with me?" And I said, "Not right now honey. I'm sorry, mommy's busy. But I promise I'll play with your children!" (*?) What kind of answer was that? I wish now I would have played more, and I regret saying that, but I can't take it back-so, now it's time to fulfill that promise.

My grandma was awesome! She always said that she didn't have favorites, BUT, I'm here to tell you, she did, AND I was it! What a great position to be in! I'm serious--I could have said to my Grandma, "Grandma, I'm sorry, but I got so mad at someone today, I just had to kill them!" Now I know this is an exaggeration, so please don't write me any letters about it. Anyway, she probably would have said, "Well honey," (she always called me honey) She'd a said, "Honey, they shouldn't have done something to make you so mad!" But let my sister just walk in the room and say, "Hi", and Grandma would say, "Don't you think you're wearing a little too much mascara?" I felt sorry for my sister, but it wasn't my fault she wasn't the favorite. I mean after all, who can blame me for being so likeable?

Grandma was always there for me, through thick and thin. I knew I could count on her. Grandma gave as much as she could while she was here, and now she has gone on to heaven, with Jesus. People are temporary. We are all terminal in this world. We're not meant to be here forever, and who really would want to?

Maybe you had someone special like my grandma, or maybe someone you loved deeply has passed on, or abandoned you in some way, and you feel all alone.

24

Well I want you to know that there is One that promises that He will never leave you nor forsake you-and that is JESUS! He promises to be with us always. He called us his friend. You've got a friend!

You just call out His name, and you know wherever you are-He'll be waiting-oh yes He will, He's not very far. Winter, Spring, Summer, or Fall, all you've got to do is call, and He'll be there. Yes, He will. You've got a friend. Ain't it good to know, you've got a friend. Oh yeah, you've got a friend.

Remember-you've got a friend. Just call His name!

Lord, HELP! My situation seems hopeless, I can't take it anymore. I need a fresh touch from You right now! Please strengthen and encourage me, as You walk with me through this. Please give me the peace and perseverance I need to press on. Thank you for never letting go. I love you Lord-thank you for being my Savior, and friend. In Jesus name, AMEN!

He really is just a call away. Isn't that a comforting thought? Knowing that we can call on His name, and He is there? He doesn't say, "Not now, I'm too busy. But I promise to be there when your children call." He really is there!

Maybe, you are going through some really tough times right now. Maybe you've lost something-a job, your health, someone you love, a dream. Or maybe you've lost all hope. If that's you-let's call on Jesus for a fresh touch of hope from Him today, knowing that He'll walk this road with you and never let go! Let's pray...

Help I Was Distracted!

"Don't forget to turn off the water to the waterbed. It's almost full," my husband called as he went out the door to work. "Yeah, okay," I mumbled, while mesmerized in front of my favorite television show. I was thinking to myself, don't bother me, I'll do it during commercial. After all, today was the big day we'd all been waiting for....Luke and Laura were finally getting married! I thought this day would never come.

My son, who was just under three and one half years old, was quietly playing with his toys. And my baby daughter, just one year old, was toddling around the room where I could keep an eye on her. I was seven months pregnant, and if felt good to sit and relax for awhile.

In case you haven't guessed, I had a serious soap opera addiction and before long I had watched one right after another, and soon a couple of hours had passed without me realizing it. All of a sudden, I remembered the water! The waterbed was still filling-OH MY GOSH!! I lurched to my feet, thoughts running through my head as to what might be awaiting me around the corner. Was there going to be water everywhere? I never heard anything. Was there going to be an explosion with a flood? I ran into the bedroom and couldn't believe my eyes. The mattress was still filling with water and it had swelled up to within a foot of the ceiling fan! I panicked and screamed, then ran outside to shut off the water. When I came back in I approached the mattress and gingerly touched it. It was as hard as a marble. It was a miracle it hadn't burst! I knew I had to get this water out of the mattress and fast-but how? I knew nothing about siphoning, but I was soon going to learn! I had watched my husband use an electric pump to drain mattresses before, so I ran and got it. I remembered it needed to be hooked up directly into the bed. That seemed simple enough. I just needed to remove the garden hose first! I was a little concerned that there might be some leakage and I didn't want water to get down inside of the bed, so I placed a towel around the area. As I pulled the hose out, the next few minutes became a blur, or should I say a gush? Water started spraying all over the room like air released from a balloon. I tried to poke the hose for the pump in, but the water just kept spraying all over me and I could hardly see. Somehow, at least, I managed to get the cap on the opening to stop the water until I could regroup.

This time, I would be better armed. I gathered some large bowls from the kitchen to help catch some of the water. Don't ask me why! How is that rational when that much water is coming out? All I can tell you is I was no longer rational at this point. I was desperate! As I approached the mattress, that now looked like "Jabba, the Hut", I became determined! I WOULD get that pump attached, no matter how wet I got! Again, I removed the cap, and as water blew out in every direction, I braved the gusher. I almost had it- it was right there, just a second longer, and then, I watched in disbelief as the pump fell from my hand as if in slow motion into the bowl full of water. There went my hope, and now I was frantic! I couldn't get the water to stop. It hit the ceiling fan which began flipping water all around the room.

My son was having a nervous breakdown, jumping up and down in the doorway while wetting his pants. The baby was in the bathroom nearby, eating toilet paper, and then gagging up wads of it on the floor. As if anything else could go wrong, the phone began to ring! I was torn between trying to stop the water flow or answering the phone and possibly getting some help- I know, another irrational thought, but it could happen. I paused for only a second and made a dash for the phone. It was my sweet little Grandmother, who lived 2 houses down from me. I didn't have time for pleasantries, so I just hollered, "HELP!!!" I heard her yell to my Grandfather to get down to my house right away and that I was having the baby!

I quickly hung up and somehow managed to reattach the garden hose to the bed. I thought to myself, if I have to suck on this thing like a straw I will. There has got to be a way to drain this! As I disconnected the hose from the outside faucet, the water began to flow freely from it, and at that moment, it clicked-that's all I would have had to have done, was disconnect the hose from the outside faucet in the first place, and it became an automatic siphon. What an idiot? How could I have been so dumb?

My Grandparents arrived, breathless, ready to help deliver my baby. I explained everything to them. They were actually relieved because they had never helped with a delivery before. Cleanup they could do. I'll never forget that day. I was a mess! My hair was sticking out all over. I was soaked from head to toe. My son was soaked from the waist down. My daughter was full of toilet paper, not to mention what the room looked like. My Grandparents and I worked to clean it all up, and you'll be happy to know that the bed did eventually return to normal size.

Did I learn a lesson from this? I sure did! 1) Always set a timer when filling a waterbed. 2) I have an ED (Experiential Degree) in siphoning in case anyone needs my services 3) There are better things to do with your time than watch soap operas! What a mess, all because I was distracted.

Sometimes, I think we're that way in our walk with the Lord. We let the attractions of this world draw our attention away from the plans and purposes of God. It may seem like it is small, but before long, it can turn into something big. And then we're in a mess. Life becomes chaotic because we have lost our focus, and it affects everyone around us. Eventually we find ourselves having to holler, HELP!!!! Oh that we would learn to keep our eyes on Jesus.

Father, sometimes the attractions of this world seem so alluring. Help us to be focused on You, that we would not be distracted from the plan You have set before us. May we learn to seek You in all things, and be the mighty people of God You have called us to be. Help us to make a difference in this world, instead of being swept up in it. Thank You for your amazing patience with us, Lord, in those times we have become distracted and You, gently, and not so gently, have brought us back. We want to be in Your will, Lord. In Jesus' name, AMEN.

"Take My Garlic Bread Please!"

One day after church, my husband Larry and I went for lunch to a nearby restaurant. We decided to order salads. We each have our own favorites, of course. The one I order comes with garlic bread, but my husband's salad does not.

Now, you have to know this, I can usually take or leave the garlic bread. However, on this particular day I was especially hungry, so I was looking forward to eating it. My husband, on the other hand, absolutely loves garlic bread. He could eat a plate of it as his dinner, and he would be thrilled.

Now we are not novices at ordering these salads. Every time we order them, Larry looks at me with surprise, and says, "You got garlic bread?"

To which I reply," Yes, my salad comes with garlic bread."

He then looks at me, with these pouty eyes, and it isn't

30

long until I give him some of my bread. Not this day. As I told you, I was extremely hungry and I don't know why I didn't think to just order a side of garlic bread. That would have been so much easier.

Instead, I was thinking to myself, "I am so hungry, and he has ordered his usual salad again and he's going to say to me, 'You got garlic bread?'" I decided that if he wanted garlic bread, then he should have ordered a salad that came with it. After all, how many times are we going to go through this? He needs to learn sometime. I guess today is the day!

Sure enough, here came the salads, and here came the look with the same question, "You got garlic bread?"

To which I replied with the same pat answer that had become so familiar, "YES, MINE COMES WITH GARLIC BREAD!"

As I was preparing to enjoy my golden brown delicious warm bread, I felt the Lord impressing upon me that I should give Larry half of my bread. Believe me, I now understand the definition of wrestling with the Lord. For the next few minutes the Lord and I were having a serious discussion. Why do I need to give him half of my garlic bread?

"Because, he is your husband."

"He should have ordered a salad that came with it!"

"He is your husband"

"But I'm really hungry!"

"He is your husband and you love him. It would be the loving thing to do."

"Oh, I guess You're right. He would be so excited, and thankful to get half of this garlic bread. Alright, I'll go ahead and do it. I can see his face now. He will be so appreciative.

So I gingerly cut the garlic bread in half. Putting the 2 pieces side by side, I noted which one was the slightly bigger half. Being the martyr that I am, I placed the slightly larger one on my husband's plate.

Silence! He kept on eating, not touching the bread. I thought, surely he noticed I placed it on his plate, but, just incase he didn't, I'd let him know.

So I gently said, "I gave you half my garlic bread."

And in between chews, he nonchalantly replied," Uh huh."

UH HUH! What kind of response was that? And the garlic bread was still laying there! What, no thank you? No acknowledgement of my sacrifice? How ungrateful! I felt like snatching back the bread, but I was now feeding on my own anger, and my appetite for food was dissipating quickly. I couldn't believe it. In my eyes, I had made an unbelievable sacrifice and he couldn't be bothered to say thank you!

I started praying that, the Lord would bind my tongue, so I wouldn't say anything hurtful before I had a chance to seek Him for wisdom and direction in this matter. We finished our lunch in silence. When we got home, he went to his chair and turned on the TV, and I proceeded upstairs for some answers as to how to best address my husband's ingratitude.

As I was praying, I felt the Lord ask me, "Why did you give Larry the garlic bread?"

I said, "Because You told me to!"

The Lord chastised me and said, "I told you to give him the garlic bread because he is your husband. I told you to give it out of your love for him. But you gave it because of how thankful he would be to you. You gave it with the wrong motivation, the wrong heart. He never asked you for it. You gave it, expecting to receive something, instead of as a sacrifice of

32

love."

WOW!! I had gone in the room clearly seeing how wrong my husband was. But I ended up weeping before the Lord and asking for forgiveness because it was now clear how wrong I was. I apologized to my husband also.

It was a great lesson. It has made me examine the things I do. What are my motives? Are they pure? Am I doing this because I genuinely care, and want to do something for someone? Or am I doing it because of the recognition I will receive?

We must all ask ourselves these questions. The Lord knows our hearts. He knows whether our service is selfless or selfish. Let's ask God to give us pure hearts and motives before Him today.

Father, You are an awesome God, and it is my desire to serve You and to be used as Your vessel. Help my heart to be pure and my motivation to be of love. Cleanse me from all selfish desires, and fill me with a spirit of servant hood. May I be a flowing river of Your love and grace to others, expecting nothing in return, motivated by love for You and You alone. In Jesus' name, Amen.

When God Says "Move"

When I first heard the Lord calling me out of my job as a cosmetologist, I couldn't believe it! What Lord? You want me to speak and write a book? I loved my job, but I love the Lord more, so my husband and I worked out our budget and realized that the only way for that to happen would be if we sold our home and downsized. Otherwise, we could not afford for me to not be working.

It would mean pinching pennies, but God said, "Move" so we decided to move. Now please hang with me through this story, because you will be amazed! We listed our home for sale in early November, and found a small lot that we liked in a nice subdivision. We purchased it and waited to start our new home until we sold our old home.

A couple of months later, a sweet family came and offered a good price and we were thrilled. There was only one slight problem-they needed to sell their home first. We accepted their offerwith the agreement that our home would stay on the market. They were confident they would have no trouble selling their home. We gave the builder our lot as a down payment and got things started on construction of our new home. We were told it would be done by June. That was great-it would be plenty of time!

Months went by and no one seemed interested in our buyer's home. We were beginning to worry. We had already envisioned having to move into an apartment and store our furniture if their house sold quickly, but now we were concerned that our home may be done and theirs still not sold. It became a growing concern. After all, it was now May-one month before our home was to be done. But on May 5th a new couple came and looked at our home and loved it. They wrote a contract immediately, and it was for more money and they had just sold their home the day before. Yippee!!

Of course we were compelled to take it. Who wouldn't be? It seemed an answer to prayer. The first couple was sadly disappointed, but understood our dilemma and released us as they hadn't received any offers on their home thus far. We were so excited. We could see that God was working this out perfectly!

Two days later, a frantic call from our realtor came in. The buyer of our new couple's home had backed out of the deal because of a huge foundational crack that was discovered! Now we were worse off than before. Our house would need to remain on the market. We still had a contract with them, with a contingency on their home selling, but since this crack had been discovered, their home was less desirable than the first couple's home. Meanwhile our new home was going up!

To top things off, May 15th was the date I felt the Lord gave me to leave the Beauty shop and I went ahead and moved forward and did that because I wanted to be obedient. I knew it didn't make sense, but I knew I needed to trust God on this.

Needless to say, my husband got very stressed. God gave me such a peace and I can't explain it, but I will say it just irritated my poor husband all the more.

We had a slight reprieve in that we were informed our new home would not be finished until the end of July. That bought a little extra time, but by now it was June and we needed the money from our home in order to pay for the new one. Then a ray of hope came-our first couple's home sold!!! But their feelings were so hurt, and they drove back by the house but decided they were no longer interested. Our realtor was beside herself, but I knew God had a plan. After all, through this whole process, I had the privilege of leading her back to the Lord and I kept telling her that God will work this all out.

We really had some bizarre things happen. One couple wanted to come and see our home a second time, and the morning they were scheduled to do that, their realtor ended up in the hospital with an emergency. They ended up waiting and eventually changed their minds. Another young couple looked at it twice and said it was perfect and they were going to go home and discuss it. After not hearing from them for 2 weeks, our realtor contacted them and learned that the man did construction work, and while working he had been blown off of a power pole and was on life support in intensive care! What more could happen???

It was now July 1st and we were to close on our new home on July 28th. Much to our dismay, we started the process for some creative financing. I began to question whether or not I even heard the voice of God in the first place. After all, I had quit my job and thought our house would be sold and I was going to be a speaker and yet nothing was happening. In fact, I had sought God-ready for action, and He had shown me I needed to spend time being His friend. I quit my job to be His friend? This was not what I had envisioned.

This was definitely a time of testing, but out of it I was

drawing closer than ever to the Lord. Three weeks passed and I really enjoyed my time with Him. I finally joyfully surrendered to Him and said that if He called me out of my job just to be His friend, then that was fine with me! And I meant it. Those were wonderful times in the Lord. When I finally got to that point, doors started opening to start speaking!

When in doubt, do the last thing God told you to do. He said, "Move", so I started packing in faith. We had been having yard sales all along and now I was boxing up everything I could get my hands on.

My husband asked, 'What are you doing? You don't even know when we'll get to move, if ever?"

But I assured him that we would be moving because God finishes what He starts!

As my husband's frustration level grew, he realized he had to surrender this to the Lord, or he was going to go crazy! When he finally did surrender, he too, was filled with a peace that passes understanding that can only come from God. With our creative financing in place we went ahead and closed on our new home. Our first house payment would be Sept. 1st.

August 1st came and we made our other house payment. Where we'd get the money for 2 house payments we didn't know, but we knew God would provide. We pressed on and went ahead and painted and hung ceiling fans in our new home and got all the things done we would have wanted to do anyway.

God is faithful and He did provide. A few days later a new couple entered the picture, wrote a cash offer on our home and wanted possession in 2 weeks. The offer was less than our original, but since we never had to move or get storage, we actually came out money ahead. It was definitely the perfection of the Lord. We never had to make 2 payments or move early, and in the meantime, I had written my story and was now approved as a speaker for an international ministry. I praise God for that! Only God could have worked out timing that excellent. He far surpassed anything we could imagine.

Through all of this our faith grew stronger and so did our realtor's and we witnessed the miracle of how God can move. It can be a scary thing to step out in obedience, but we walk by faith and not by sight. We must trust in the Lord with all of our hearts and lean not on our own understanding. *Joshua 1:9, "Have I not commanded you? Be strong and of good courage; do not be afraid, nor be dismayed, for the Lord your God is with you wherever you go."* We can walk in confidence knowing that God is in control. No matter how bleak your circumstances may look, just keep doing what He's called you to do. Obedience is the key to success.

Lord,

I want to be obedient to Your will. Strengthen my faith to trust You more and more. To move when You say move, and wait when You say wait. Your timing is more excellent than anything I could begin to put together. Help me to let go and let You handle all the details. Forgive me, Lord for the times I have tried to do things in my own strength and take control. I know that if I seek first Your kingdom and Your righteousness, that You will add all the other things I need. Thank You, Lord, for loving me so! In Jesus' name, AMEN.

"What Bitterness Breeds"

Have you ever been angry at anyone? Maybe someone has done something that has made you mad or hurt you in some way, and you became offended and bitter. I HAVE!!!

My anger was directed at my ex-husband. I am not proud of it now, but I remember a time in my life when the bitterness I felt bred an idea in me that I thought was the answer to my problem! I am not kidding...are you ready for this???

"The Ex-Husband Piñata Kit" That's right!! I had it all figured out. I was going to make millions off of this baby! I would patent it, and there was no doubt in my mind that it would sell like wildfire. Now you all know what a piñata is, right? They are very popular in Mexico. They're made out of paper mache, and usually shaped like an animal. You fill them with candy and then hang them up, just out of reach. The children line up and take turns one at a time, swinging a stick while blindfolded, trying to hit the piñata, until one of them finally breaks it open and they all get the candy!

But as my bitterness kept breeding-it did not stop there. My husband, Larry, also had 2 ex-wives. They could get on my nerves, too. So why limit this kit to only ex-husbands. How about "The Ex-Spouse Piñata Kit"? That will sell EVEN MORE!!!

I told my husband-"Honey we will be rich! We'll put faces in the kit, like Mr. and Mrs. Potato Head. There will be different colors of hair and hairdo's. Of course, if they are bald, you just don't put the hair on.

I could just see it! Then, we would include some self stick letters so that they could put their names on them, or whatever "term of endearment" they desired. Of course with the technology now, they could actually generate a picture for the face and just paste it on!

I was so excited and the more I thought of this, the more I could picture it-and that just kept adding fuel to the fire. The ideas were rolling in for marketing of my ingenious invention. My only hesitation was wondering what to fill it with? I thought about money, but I really didn't have much money to be filling it with. In fact, that was part of what started my bitterness to begin with. Of course, I knew I would have some money after I started selling these little beauties. I could always fill it with dirty socks! Those always seem to be plentiful.

Once the piñata is made, and filled, you invite over your closest friends for a party. You know, the ones that you have nursed and rehearsed your story with so that now the bitterness has passed on to them as well? You have a few munchies, sit around and rehash everything so it's fresh in everyone's minds. Then you get a "BIG STICK," and you all beat the tar out of the piñata! I thought, "Isn't this idea great?"

After all, I couldn't actually beat them in person. I didn't really want to do that anyway. Besides, I'd get arrested. So, this was the answer. After all, they deserved it. They were trying to make my life miserable. But I'd show them. I'd turn it all around, and make money to boot!

Thank God-The Lord rescued me from my bitterness. The Bible says in: *Hebrews 12:15 See to it that no one comes short of the grace of God; that no root of bitterness springing up causes trouble, and by it many be defiled.* Look at how my bitterness could have spilled onto many others all through my actions. Whether they deserved it was not the point.

What if God gave us what we deserve? That's a scary thought! Thank God He doesn't. We would all perish-end of story! But He has grace for us because He loves us so much. He sent His son Jesus to die for us so we can be forgiven. Do you realize what that means? He took the punishment for us! He took the punishment for you!

We deserve to be a piñata, but through faith in Christ, instead of beating us, He carries us. Instead of keeping from us, He provides for us. Instead of hating us, He loves us. And, instead of condemning us, He forgives us.

In Ephesians 4:31-32 it says: Let all bitterness and wrath and anger and clamor and slander be put away from you, along with all malice. Be kind to one another, tenderhearted, forgiving each other, just as God in Christ also has forgiven you.

Maybe you are struggling today with some unresolved bitterness. Don't let it keep breeding in your life. Jesus said in *Matthew 6:14-15 "For if you forgive others for their transgressions, your heavenly Father will also forgive you. But if you do not forgive others, then your Father will not forgive your transgressions."*

You may be thinking, "You don't know my situation. I have a right to be angry. You don't realize what I've been through!"

41

Or, maybe you're thinking, "I know I should forgive, but I just can't right now."

Let's ask God to start the process right now of healing your heart and mind, and freeing you from this choke hold on your life. Will you pray with me?

Lord,

Thank you for not giving me what I deserve. Thank you for the blood of Jesus that cleanses me. Father, please change my heart. The hurt is so deep and I can't do it on my own. Please root out all of the bitterness that has been growing there. Heal and restore me. Give me strength, and a spirit of forgiveness towards others. Cloak me with humility. May I not be proud or arrogant, knowing that it's only by Your grace that I am forgiven. Thank you for loving me so much! In Jesus name, AMEN!

"Why the Mustache?"

The Bible says because of sin, women will experience severe pain in childbirth. There is also a lot of pain leading up to that point I might add, but I can understand it. It all has a purpose.

I made it through the cramps, PMS, stretch marks and labor. And, as painful as it was, it was all worth it. I have 3 beautiful children. After I had experienced all these things, it looked like clear sailing in the physical appearance department. I had gotten rid of all my extra weight from childbirth. I was body building, lifting weights, and my skin was a beautiful golden brown from tanning. Everything was looking good except for a little mustache that was gradually becoming more noticeable. It soon became more than just noticeable!

Why doesn't someone tell you," Oh by the way, when you're all done having babies, you get to grow a mustache! And if you're really lucky, you may get one sooner!" At least you'd have some warning!

I had NO mustache experience. What do you do with it? Now, I know that there are a select few of you who don't have to deal with this. If you are one of them, consider yourself blessed! My husband has a mustache, and I love it, on him! I didn't want one of my own! But that's what I got! I was afraid if I shaved it, I'd end up with whiskers! I needed advice as to what to do. So I checked with a well known makeup/modeling agency. Their advice was to bleach it. They said it would blend right in and no one would even notice it.

Great idea! So I purchased some facial hair bleach- no not Clorox, and I locked myself in the bathroom to be alone. I applied the foamy mixture to my mustache. Whew-this stuff was stinky and it felt like it was burning out my nose hairs. My eyes were watering, but that's okay, it would be well worth it! When the processing time was up, I carefully rinsed it and Voila!, a blonde mustache! WOW! Is that less noticeable? With my tanned skin, I wasn't so sure. Maybe no one will notice.

I opened the bathroom door just in time for my precious 4 year old daughter to round the corner and catch a glimpse of me. She was excited as she exclaimed, "Mommy, you look like Hulk Hogan!" Now granted, to her that was a compliment, after all, Hulk Hogan was her favorite wrestler. He was very muscular, with bronzed skin, beautiful blonde hair and a matching mustache to go with it.

That is it! No more mustache! It's coming off no matter what! So I purchased some facial wax strips and started waxing it off. Through the years I began to grow more confident in what I was doing. I started to question why the directions said not to shower before using. After all, it seemed to me that since you had to clean the area before applying the strip anyway, it just made more sense to shower first. I soon learned however, that when you do that, the water softens your skin so much that then the wax pulls your skin right off. Then, instead of a mustache, you have a big scab. It looks like a carpet burn on your lip! Try explaining that when someone asks you what happened!

You would think I would learn after once, but, oh no. I can be a little slow in that department. So, when the instructions said DO NOT reapply immediately after using, you know what I did? After all, some of the hair had not removed, and it seemed like way too much effort to tweeze it as the directions had indicated. And being the expert that I was (of course, I knew more than the makers of the product), again, I did it my way. Oh I was an expert all right-an expert at acquiring scabs!

That's something I want to ask when I get to heaven. Why Lord? Why the mustache? What were you thinking? I don't understand it. I have yet to see a purpose for it! Were you just feeling humorous that day or what?

We all have "why" questions. This one happens to be a humorous one, but many of us have some that aren't so funny. Maybe you are wrestling with some serious "why" questions that have caused you a great amount of pain. I won't even presume to be able to answer them. All I can do is to encourage you with *Proverbs 3:5, which says; Trust in the Lord with all your heart, and lean not on your own understanding. In all your ways acknowledge Him, and He shall direct your paths.* We are to trust God, and not lean on our

Lord,

We come to You today with heavy hearts. Hearts that cry out and question things that have happened that we don't understand. Things that have caused us such grief and pain, that seem more than we can bear. In our frailty, at times, we tend to look back and wonder why. Forgive us, oh Lord. Help us to stop taking things into our own hands, and start placing everything in Yours. May we learn to trust You in every circumstance. Thank You for walking this road with us, and for never letting go. In Jesus' name, Amen.

45

understanding, and He will direct us. God's ways don't always make sense to us, and that's okay. We don't have to understand it all right now. God is our Maker and He knows His product, and we must trust that. One day it will make sense, but for now we must trust and obey.

He promises us in that He works ALL things together for good for those that love Him and are called according to His purpose. ALL things, not SOME things. So let's leave it ALL in His hands and trust, that He is doing exactly that!

"I'd Rather Take the Beating"

I'm not bragging when I say that growing up, my sisters and I were pretty tough! It's the truth. Don't get me wrong, we were nice girls. However years of fighting with each other had helped to hone our skills at defending ourselves and those we loved.

We moved to Arizona when I was in the sixth grade. My Aunt and Uncle had already lived in Arizona for a couple of years, so my cousins were already well established in school. We moved during the Christmas break, so I started school there virtually in the middle of the year.

Imagine my horror when I learned that everyday my little 5th grade cousin was being beaten up during lunch recess. You already had to feel sorry for him, as he was the only boy in our family in this state. That was bad enough, and to top it off, they thought he had a hearing problem so he had started wearing a hearing aid. I don't know if he really did have trouble hearing, or if he had just mastered the art of tuning us all out, but at any rate, he had one. I found out that he had been having some problems with some kids at school, but he had been given strict instructions that under no circumstances was he ever to hit anyone-self defense or not! Well, of course, when the other kids found out about this, they enjoyed nothing better than taunting him even more, and eventually beating him to a pulp knowing he wouldn't defend himself. It had become a daily occurrence at the lunch recess, and it made me furious.

I thought to myself, I didn't grow up with that rule, so it was "super cousin" to the rescue. I could almost hear singing as I marched over to the playground to the tune of "Here comes Sherry to save the day!" There was my cousin, lying on the ground, with these bullies kicking him as he tried to stay curled in a ball to avoid injury. This was ridiculous, so I made quick work of the situation! I cleaned all of their clocks, and then issued a warning before I left. 'Don't make me come back here, he is my cousin, and I will not hesitate to do this again if I need to. I don't care who it is, boys or girls!' Done, that should take care of it. There should be no more problems for my cousin. He would be so grateful, and that would be all the thanks I needed.

When school got out I couldn't wait to hear his praise and adoration for my intervention. He came stomping up to me and proclaimed with disgust," Thanks a lot!"

What do you mean? I can't believe he is not elated.

He went on to say," Since you came over and beat up those boys-now all the kids are saying I had to have a girl come and save me."

"But I thought I was helping you," I protested.

"I'd rather take the beating," he sneered.

Thus ended my fighting career, and any future hope at a title, other than the girl who could beat up boys! I'll take it!

Funny how often times we think we are helping someone or something, only to learn we've made matters worse. Like the story of the butterfly and how a man saw it struggling to break out of its cocoon. He decided to help it by cutting open the cocoon so it could get out, only later discovering that he had actually crippled it, because it's in the struggle that the wings become strong enough to fly!

That happens in life, too. We want to help someone out of a difficult situation. And there is nothing wrong with that. But there are times when the struggle needs to happen so they can become strong. It's in the struggle that we see God and become stronger in the Lord. Or it may be the struggle that actually opens our eyes and helps us to see our need for Him. We need to pray and seek God in every situation. We should help when He calls us to, and we should step back when He says," This struggle will make them strong."

Maybe you are going through a struggle right now and you don't seem to be getting much help. Trust that God knows what He is doing. Hang in there, and you'll come through it stronger for doing so!

James 1:2-4 My brethren, count it all joy when you fall into various trials, knowing that the testing of your faith produces patience. But let patience have its perfect work, that you may be perfect and complete, lacking nothing.

Father,

I'm growing and sometimes it's hard. When I struggle I don't always like it, but I can have peace knowing that You will make me strong through it. Help me to trust each step of the way as You mold and shape me into something useful for fulfilling Your purposes. The character process isn't always sweet, but it's necessary to complete, so give me joy in the process and I will be strengthened in You. In Jesus' name, AMEN.

Going Through the Motions

When my son was a young boy, he wanted to be in the band at school. At that time, the earliest you could start was in fifth grade. He wanted to play the saxophone, but we didn't have much money, so consequently, buying or renting the instrument was not an option. So, we checked with the school to see what was available at no cost. Well it wasn't a saxophone like he'd hoped. Instead, it was the French horn. Apparently, there wasn't a huge demand for a French horn. Since he was so anxious to be in the band, he agreed to play it. It was quite a sight, watching my little boy trying to ride his bicycle back and forth to school, with this big French horn almost toppling him over, but he was determined!

Practicing, however, was a whole other story! Oh, how he hated to practice, and I'll be honest, when they are first learning, it can be excruciating to listen to! He had always been that way from little on up. He wanted to play a sport, but he just wanted to play the game. He didn't want to bother with practicing or learning the basics!

I would continually remind him to practice his horn, and he would tell me he had, and I would believe him. In fact, I was at times relieved that he had practiced, and somehow, I had missed out on the joy of hearing it.

Finally, after months, it came time for the big concert at school. This one would be held in an auditorium. That somehow made it seem more prestigious. He would need a new outfit, shirt, tie, dress pants, and shoes. The big night finally arrived. His hair was all slicked back. He was so handsome, and looked all grown up. My little boy, up on stage, playing in a concert. I was a proud mama! We took lots of pictures, and when the concert was over, we had him pose on the stage and took more pictures of him with his instrument. We had some friends whose daughter was also in the band, so we took their pictures together. It really was a memorable occasion!

A couple of days after the concert, my son came and said he didn't want to be in the band anymore. What??? My son, whose name I had already envisioned in lights, his career was just starting, now wants to quit-why? He told me he didn't like it, and when I reminded him of the wonderful concert, he confessed to me that he hadn't actually played in the concert. Apparently, he hadn't ever really practiced much, and therefore didn't know how to play the French horn. So the teacher had kindly asked him to just pretend to be playing. Just puff out his cheeks, and push the buttons, but don't blow! He was just going through the motions. I couldn't believe it-all this time he was just pretending! Instead of a future famous concert player, we had our own little "Milli Vanilli" band boy, with plenty of pictures to prove it. Milli Vanilli was a popular vocal team at one time, until it was later discovered that they never actually sang any of the songs they performed. They had lip-synced everything. They had pretended---again, simply gone through the motions.

I've started wondering, how many people are going through life pretending? How many have cleaned themselves up-go to church-go through the motions- lip-sync the gospel---do all the right things while others are watching, but deep inside there has never been a transformation of the heart? They've played the part-the game-without knowing the basics-- the Savior? They're pretenders or hypocrites. And the Bible says no hypocrite will enter the Kingdom of Heaven.

And sadly, there are many like that, who are merely reading the notes on the page instead of participating in the symphony.

If that is you, God wants you to know Him, intimately. You can't pretend, because God sees your heart. Don't just go through the motions. Repent-and let Jesus transform the empty halls of your heart with the music of His presence, and live a life of praise for Him!

Oh Lord, it is my desire to live the life you have called me to live, with joy and expectancy! I want to experience the melody You have written for me. Forgive me, Lord, for the sins that I have committed and come and fill every crevice of my heart with Your presence. I want to make music with You all the days of my life. I trust You, knowing that You will be with me through the high and low notes of life. Thank you for not giving up on me. I look forward to my new life today, complete in You! In Jesus' name, Amen

Blown Off Blessings

Some of my favorite memories as a child are camping trips in Wisconsin. It was such great fun! We had two favorite places. One was a lake with a heavily wooded area for camping and hiking, and the other had lush tree filled camping spots, with a river nearby. We had a red and white striped tent camper. It looked like a candy cane, so there was no mistaking which camp was ours! My Dad had a friend from work, and he and his family loved to camp also, so we experienced many trips together. We grew very close to them so that makes the memories that much sweeter. Of course as a bonus, they also had 3 children, so we had someone to play with, 2 of them were boys-Yee ha! I loved every minute of it, from waking up in the morning with the smell of bacon and eggs my Dad was cooking, to hiking and exploring in the woods, fishing and playing in the water, and the treats over the campfire each night, consisting of roasted marshmallows, smores, hot fruit pies and Jiffy popcorn! Nothing tasted better than Jiffy popcorn cooked over the fire! To top it off, all the Fresca I could drink: I was a huge Fresca fan!

You can imagine my delight when I learned that the man of my dreams also loved to camp and fish, and I could hardly wait for my children to experience what I had. However camping as a child and camping as an adult are two different things. The trip definitely has a different flavor to it. It's called WORK! There are things to pack, equipment to load, food to buy and prepare, the work to setup camp, then work to pack up, all the unloading, and lest we forget, a mound of laundry! Where was all that fun I remembered? I eventually learned however, through experience I might add, not to go camping and take the kids, when my husband was fishing a tournament weekend, because at those times, his version of camping was drastically different from mine! Now don't get me wrong, we did have fun. We took some trips that were incredible, but for the for the most part, it was always the same scenario...Pull up close to the lake, but don't unhook the boat to set up camp, as you have to get up at 4 am to back it into the water. As far as trees, there were NO trees. Oh yea-this was Arizona, we're talking desert! No trees for miles, just a little scrub brush or two once in awhile. No bathrooms, that's what the scrub brush were for. Campfires were made in the dirt, but they didn't last long as morning would come early and there was fish to be caught! My husband along with the other men in the club would fish all day, then weigh the fish and turn them loose. We'd cook dinner, cleanup, a little fire time with fish stories, and off to bed to start the whole process over again the next day. After that, the tournament would be over and it would be time to pack up and go. The kids would wait expectantly, hoping to go fishing, or at least have a ride in the boat, but by then my husband was usually too tired, and just wanted to get home. They would be so disappointed. Once in a while, if they were lucky, they might talk him into a quick ride. We made the most of it, the kids and me. We'd set up a shade canopy and make a little camp. We'd play games and they would play in the water and look for shells. We'd eat snacks. There was no place to hike, like I said it was desert, unless you count the hike to the scrub brush off in the distance when you needed to go to the bathroom! Now that was an adventure-watching out for rattlesnakes. Sometimes, some of the other men's families would come along and that would give the kids someone to play with during the day and me someone else to talk to. Our final trip to the lake, none of the other families came, so we experienced it all on our own. The kids and I fondly refer to it as the trip from HELL!

It was Chad's birthday so he had invited his cousin along. I'm not clear on the kid's ages but I think my son was about 10 and the girls were 7 and 8. I do remember it was the middle of the summer and that I will never forget!

The fun started the minute we got there. It was already dark and the girls were running around with flashlights and discovered some adorable little scorpions right in the area where we were preparing to camp, so we had to move. My husband was gracious and set up the shade canopy that night and we got our cozy little camp all set up. I must say it looked quite comfortable. The girls were small, but girls always have a lot of stuff, and since there were three of them they shared the bigger tent. Chad and his cousin were in the smaller tent. They were a little too big for it, so part of their bodies stuck out, but they didn't care. They could look at the stars. My husband and I were in the pickup bed that had a little camper shell on it. We were accompanied by Dinky, our little dog. Not the most luxurious accommodations, but doable for the weekend. The night was quiet as we nestled down and rested peaceful-ly-that is until a horrific storm blew in. The wind kicked up with a huge dust storm, followed by pelting rain with thunder and lightning that cracked with a vengeance. The girls were terrified, their tent was rocking back and forth and they want-ed out, but that would have been more dangerous than staying put. We told them to each lay in a corner of the tent so it wouldn't blow away, and they would be all right. They crawled in the corners and laid there and screamed! We tried to grab the perishables and throw them in the camper shell, but it was difficult to get everything. We were getting drenched! My son and his cousin, without much protection, had already climbed into the cab of the truck, one in the front seat, the other in the back. The dog was hyperventilating in the camper, with the water logged items we had managed to rescue. All we could do was wait it out. Thankfully the storm didn't last long, but long enough to do some serious damage. The shade tarp had blown off, that much we knew, but as for anything else, we'd have to wait until morning to survey the damage. Our poor little girls had screamed themselves to sleep.

Four o'clock came early and the fishing tournament began. As I surveyed the destruction, it looked hopeless. Even though we had saved the boxes of cereal, the dishes were all full of dirt and water. The shade canopy had actually ripped and there was no fixing it-it was ruined, and already the temperature was beginning to climb. The table and chairs, along with all of our equipment, was covered with mud. Everything was soaked including our paper towels, so we used beach towels to wipe things off. You can imagine how dirty those became. I glazed the kids down heavily with sunscreen several times through out the day. We did pretty well considering the circumstances, but soon grew weary from being in the sun that long. The heat was getting to us. The kids had played in the water until they were prunes, and couldn't take it anymore, and by 3 pm, with no shade and 115 degrees, we were all burnt to a crisp. Periodically we would get in the truck and turn on the air conditioner, but without the vehicle moving, it was just hot air, so that was useless. There were other vehicles parked around us, so we couldn't drive anywhere. We were hot, tired, cranky, and desperate for shade. Praise the Lord for the dog. She was panting and miserable but she managed to find a cooler spot and we marveled at her ingenuity. She had crawled under the truck where the only shade existed for miles. We all soon joined her! Who cared that we were lying on the dirt that the night before had scorpions. It was shade-glorious shade!

After that, I decided I was done camping at the lake, and the kids and I never went along again! When our children grew older and became adults, one of them asked me,"Hey Mom, why did we ever quit going to the lake?" Before I could respond, they realized and said,"Oh yeah, I remember." Me too!

As I thought about that trip, I realized that one bad experience kept me from enjoying any future ones. Sometimes I think we as Christians are like that when we are new in the Lord. Everything is wonderful. God is blessing us and it's a great time in our lives. We are a new creation in Christ. But as we walk out our salvation with fear and trembling, we eventually have to walk through some difficult experiences- or some tribulation. Sometimes we give up, and decide this walk isn't worth the heartache. We forget the previous blessings and miss out on future ones because of our refusal to go any further. It makes me think of the Israelites and how one minute they were praising God for releasing them from bondage and the next minute they were ready to go back to Egypt as slaves again, because they thought it would be easier.

How many wonderful times have I missed out on because of this one bad experi-

Lord,

You bless me so much each and every day and yet when the going gets tough, I am sometimes tempted to turn away. Help my judgment not to be swayed by bad experiences. Thank You for Your mercies that, are new every morning. You are able to do far greater things than I could ever dream or imagine. I don't want to miss out on anything You have planned for me. Help me not blow off my future blessings. My life, hope and strength are in You Lord. In Jesus' name, AMEN.

57

ence, and I could ask you the same thing? Have you gotten frustrated and turned your back on God because of a bad experience you've had? Maybe you've been hurt by someone who professed to be a Christian? Maybe you've felt abandoned by the Lord? Let me encourage you... His mercies are new every morning! New means He has a brand new batch everyday and they are sufficient for whatever you are going through. Don't blow off the blessings because of a bad experience, and risk missing the call of God on your life.

How Soon
We Forget

My husband and I were in the mall the other day, shopping for our grandson's birthday present. Now every woman knows how little most men like to shop. I must commend my husband, though, because under the circumstances, he did quite well. In fact, he did better than me!

As we walked through the children's department, little bodies would dart in and out of the aisles in front of us. They were chasing each other through the store as the faint voice of the mother was heard, warning them to stop! As we neared the cash register with our purchase, it grew worse. Here was the mother-not one, but two of them, shopping together. They had brought their little darlings along. Wasn't that special? Their children were running circles around the register, with the exception of one little girl, with "Princess" on her shirt. She had just stuck out her tongue and kicked one of the little boys in front of us. Another little boy ran around hollering and picking on the other children, while the mother would calmly say,

"Tommy, that's enough", while still focused on paying for her items. "Tommy, that's not nice. Please quit doing that." Seconds later..."Tommy, I said that's enough." That was enough all right-in my eyes. That was enough talk time for Tommy! I was ready for SHOWTIME!

As my husband and I left, our nerves frazzled, I thought to myself...Have I grown old and crabby, or were those children just brats? I found myself wondering why people bring their children to the mall, and yet I did that very same thing. Granted, my children are all grown now, but I always took them to the store and thought nothing of it. How soon we forget what it was like. After all, one of my shopping experiences with my children forced me to put my son on a leash from then on. I know, you're probably thinking, how cruel, a leash, that's for dogs. I will admit, I did get a lot of stares and comments, but I didn't care. When you have three small children and only two hands, you must use every resource available to insure that you don't lose them. I didn't worry about what the other people thought because, after all, they weren't there for one of my life's most embarrassing moments. If they were, they would have been using a leash too! You may be asking, "Why on earth were you shopping with three small children?" To tell you the truth, I really don't remember, but I do remember this!

I had finally found a parking space, and proceeded to get the big double stroller out from the back of the van. In those days, strollers didn't just open with the push of a button. It was work to unfold them and make sure everything was secure before putting a child inside. Once it was ready, I carefully placed my 2 month old daughter into the front of the stroller in her infant seat. That left just enough room for my 16mo. old daughter to sit in the back of it. Once they were strapped in and secure, I got my 3 1/2 year old son, Chad, out of his car seat and had him walk with me into the department store. I wrestled with the door, which wasn't automatic, since there was no one around to help. My son entered first, and I finally got the stroller inside. I was going to look at the clothes in front of me when I realized that Chad was not there. As I frantically looked around, I saw him spinning around in the clothing rack. I hollered at him, and headed in his direction. He thought this was a great game, and he ran towards the dressing rooms. I couldn't believe what transpired next. Just as quick as a wink, he lay down on his back, and scooted himself under one of the occupied fitting rooms. Before I could grab him, he hollered out, "Ooh, hairy!" I thought I would die! I was mortified! Needless to say, we left immediately! I didn't want to see the poor woman that was in there. I'd never be able to look her in the face. For that matter, I'm sure she didn't want to see anyone either. I've often wondered if she ever did come out!

So before I pass judgment on some poor mother at the mall, I must remember what it was like.

I think we get that way as Christians sometimes, too. We forget what it was like-how we were before we accepted Jesus as our Savior. It becomes easy for us to pass judgment on the world, and yet, were it not for the grace of God, we would still be in our sin.

Ephesians 2:1-7 And you He made alive, who were dead in trespasses and sins, in which you once walked according to the course of this world, according to the prince of the power of the air, the spirit who now works in the sons of disobedience, among whom also we all once conducted ourselves in the lusts of our flesh and of the mind, and were by nature children of wrath, just as the others. But God, who is rich in mercy, because of His great love with which He loved us, even when we were dead in trespasses, made us alive together with Christ (by grace you have been saved), and raised us up together, and made us sit together in the heavenly places in Christ Jesus, that in the ages to come He might show the exceeding riches of His grace in His kindness toward us in Christ Jesus.

Where would we be if someone had not shown us our need for a Savior? And we must do the same. We must not pass judgment, but out of gratitude for the grace of God, share the gospel with the children of wrath. God doesn't want anyone to perish, but all to come to repentance. Without Jesus they will experience the wrath of God on Judgment Day! We must help to seek and save the lost! We must come off of our complacent cozy couches and spread the gospel to every creature. We must let compassion swallow our fear. I thank God someone did that for me!

Lord, thank You for pulling me up out of the miry clay! Help me not to judge others, but instead share You with them. Remind me of where I've been, and where I would have been if not for Your incredible grace. Use that memory to quicken me to share the gospel with everyone I come into contact with. Free me from all fear to boldly declare Your truth. May I be a beacon of Your light that shines so brightly that it ignites a fire that will start a blaze of revival within Your church. In Jesus' name, AMEN

If You Play With Fire . . .

You've heard it said that curiosity killed the cat? Well thankfully our daughter isn't a cat, but she definitely was curious. At fourteen years of age, she was home alone one night, while the rest of us were out for the evening at different events. She had lit a candle in the family room where she was watching television, and there was a pencil lying nearby along with a paper towel. Apparently, it seemed very inviting to take the pencil and stick it into the flame. So, seeking to satisfy her curiosity, she poked and prodded the pencil in the flame of the candle until her pencil eventually became a hot coal. Needing to dispose of it, she wrapped it in the paper towel to avoid dropping ashes on the carpet while carrying it to the kitchen. You guessed it! The paper towel caught on fire. So, what did she do? She reasoned that you blow on a candle to put it out, so that's what she did. She blew on the paper towel. No, I am not kidding! That was the wrong thing to do! It ignited in her hands! She bravely hung onto it and ran into the bathroom and threw it in the sink but not before she was severely burned! I have said that her sacrifice saved our home, but the other kids are quick to point out that if she hadn't been playing with the fire, there would have been no danger to begin with. True!

When this happened, she was unable to reach us, so when we got home I went in to check on her and found her lying in her bed whimpering, with both her hands in a bowl of ice water. She was trying to sleep but the pain was too great.

The burns were serious and I ended up taking her to the emergency room. Several hours later, we were on our way home with pain medications, creams and both of her hands completely bandaged due to the severity of the burns. She looked like she had on white boxing gloves. I'm happy to say that she eventually healed and is fine, but she no longer pokes pencils in candles!

You know what? As Christians we're that way sometimes too! The Lord has given specific instructions as to things we are to stay away from, and yet sometimes we think if we just dabble in them a little, what can it hurt? Us! When we open doors to things the Lord has forbidden, we are actually giving the devil a foothold in our life. And, anytime the devil is involved, you can count on getting burned.

Deuteronomy 18:10-14, "There shall not be found among you anyone who makes his son or his daughter pass through the fire, or one who practices witchcraft, or a soothsayer, or one who interprets omens or a sorcerer, or one who conjures spells, or a medium, or a spiritist, or one who calls up the dead. For all who do these things are an abomination to the Lord, and because of these abominations the Lord your God drives them out from before you. You shall be blameless before the Lord your God. "For these nations which you dispossess listened to soothsayers and diviners; but as for you, the Lord your God has not appointed such for you.

This is just a portion of the things that the Lord specifically forbids. There are many others, but scripture makes it clear that we are not to consult with psychics, or astrology-- horoscopes, or anything else that has to do with the occult such as ouigie boards, taro cards, séances, hypnotism, yoga, or transcendental meditation-just to name a few. The world makes them seem so inviting and harmless, but they are not! They are definitely of the devil, and he is trying to lure you around every corner. They are advertised on television, in newspapers, magazines and they have begun to seem the norm.

I fear for the people who profess to be Christians and see nothing wrong with experiencing these things. Take this as a warning. Don't test God on this. If we love God, we will obey what He has commanded. If you have opened any doors like this in your life to the devil, shut them down immediately, renounce them and repent before the Lord. Satan can only have a foothold in your life if you let him! Trust me, if you play with fire-you will get burned!

Lord,

You have made it clear in Your word what is acceptable and pleasing to You and what is an abomination. Father, I long to be found faithful at Your return. I renounce and repent of things I have dabbled in that You have commanded me not to. Forgive me, Lord, for my disobedience and cleanse me from all unrighteousness. Lord, I pray that as I seek You, no weapon formed against me shall prosper, and I ask that You put a protective hedge around me and my family. Thank You for this wake up call to the scheme of the enemy. To You be the glory! In Jesus name, AMEN.

65

"Expect the Unexpected"

Let me just tell you that when you work as a hairdresser in a nursing home for eleven years, you learn to expect the unexpected! I could tell you stories for days of some of the experiences I've had. It was an awesome time in my life and the people were precious-but there were some days...

One time in particular, still makes me laugh every time it comes to mind. First, I need to give you a brief update on three clients. I shampooed and set these ladies' hair every week, so I became very familiar with their behavior. Violet (nicknamed Faye) had suffered a debilitating stroke that left her without the ability to communicate. She could say the word "yes", but other than that her vocabulary was limited to "debe, debe, debe." Of course, not being able to communicate well was extremely frustrating for her. She also had a short temper, and it didn't take a rocket scientist to know when she was becoming irritated with you. She would say, "debe, debe, debe" several times with each syllable growing louder and angrier. That was the cue to look out! Many times she would grow impatient and decide she was finished getting her hair done-right in the middle of the process. She would begin ripping rollers out of her hair and if you tried to stop her, she would pinch or try to bite you. One thing she despised was for anyone to talk to me while she was in there, whether it be in the doorway or on the telephone. She would not tolerate it. She would become violent. At times like that, I thought of her as Violent Violet!

Then there was Emma. Dear sweet Emma-she usually fell asleep under the dryer, and try as she might, she just couldn't keep her head up. I would have to go over and awaken her every few minutes to put her head back under the dryer, otherwise her hair would not dry. Awakening Emma had to be done delicately, because if she became startled, this could result in a bloodcurdling scream that could last for over fi hour. And last, but not least, there was Evelyn. Now Evelyn had multiple personalities, so you were never sure who you would be dealing with. It could change at any moment. At times, she was so sweet, and would refer to me as honey, and at other times, this deep man's voice would boom out of her accusing me of stealing her boyfriend, Sir Lancelot. When Evelyn was in the beauty shop, needless to say, there was never a dull moment.

This particular day, I had Emma under the dryer, sleeping of course, and I had continued diligently to wake her up every few minutes so her hair would dry. Her hair was very thick, and it took a long time to dry anyway, but at this rate it would be all day! I had just put little Faye under the other dryer, and all was well. For five minutes that is! After that, Faye decided her hair was dry, and she flipped the dryer hood back and started rolling towards the door. I went and got her, while sweetly explaining to her that it would be just a little longer. I was able to coax her back under the dryer, oops, time to reawaken Emma, and adjust her head. Now, it was Evelyn's turn to have her hair done, while the other ladies were drying. I started washing her hair-stop---coax Faye back under---awaken Emma-resume washing. Finally, it was time to start setting Evelyn's hair-stop-coax Faye again-awaken Emma. This had become a routine. Just when I thought we were almost home free, the phone rang. It was a customer from the apartments wanting to make an appointment. This customer was very hard of hearing, and I had to repeat everything loudly several times. That was it! Faye had finally had enough! She became infuriated! With attitude, she flipped back the dryer hood and began to roll. I was trying to coax her while on the phone, but she would have none of it. She swung at me and out the door she went, and down the hall she headed-rollers still in her hair! I couldn't go after her, because the lady on the phone couldn't make out what I was saying when I asked her to hold on. I had an escapee, and there was nothing I could do about it until I was able to hang up. Just then, Evelyn burst out singing in a loud deep bravado," MINE EYES HAVE SEEN THE GLORY OF THE COMING OF THE LORD!" As she was singing, I heard a click, click, click, and looked down just in time, to see Emma's false teeth skipping across the floor! She was sleeping and her mouth had dropped open and out they came. I couldn't take it anymore. The hilarity of the moment got to me, and I broke down in laughter.

I think God knew I needed a laugh that day, so He obliged me!

Life is sometimes like that, isn't it? Things happen all around us that we have no control over and we can let it frustrate us and those around us, or

Lord, Thank You for the gift of laughter. Help me to learn to laugh at my situations more, and to complain less. May I view each as an opportunity from You to practice taking the little things in my life less serious. When my heart is fixed on You, Lord, all those little nuisances don't seem to matter. May the joy that You've poured in me, also pour forth from me! In Jesus' name, AMEN

68

we can laugh!

Proverbs 17:22 "A merry heart does good, like medicine, but a broken spirit dries the bones."

So expect the unexpected, and laugh! It really is good for you:

He's My Son

Two things I've learned…discipleship is costly and parenting isn't for sissies! Both are battlegrounds, but be strong and courageous. They are battles worth fighting, and you will come out stronger in the end. You will get battered, bruised, cut, and kicked. It will be painful. Get some knee pads. You'll need them. You will need to spend a lot of time on your knees. One day, you'll be sailing along in parenting heaven, where you can do no wrong in the eyes of your child, and suddenly IT happens! Tah Tah Tah Tah! The teenage years hit and poof! They lose their brain. BUT, the funny part is, they don't realize it's gone. After all, they now know everything. In fact, they're sure you've lost yours! The Bible says that children are a blessing from the Lord, and they truly are, but when you're going through the battle it's hard to stay focused on the blessing.

I became a Christian when my son was 14 years old, right smack dab in the middle of those precious teenage years. Jesus radically changed my life. This was a shock to my childrens' delicate little systems. I was on a mission. Time was short, and there was so much I had failed to teach them. I was hungry to know Jesus more and more, and I was desperate for my family to know Him too! I prayed, I sang, I studied, and I learned that Jesus was to be first in my life over anyone or anything-including my family. Jesus said in *Matthew 10:37-38*, *"He who loves father or mother more than Me is not worthy of Me; and he who loves son or daughter more than Me is not worthy of Me. And he who does not take his cross and follow after Me is not worthy of Me.* WOW, that's a hard one. But Jesus said it, so I wanted to follow it. I said, "I will carry my cross and follow You, Lord. I want to be Your disciple, no matter the cost!" Little did I realize that I would soon understand just how costly discipleship could be.

One night, my son, now 16, came to me and said he wanted to go and live with his dad. His father and I were divorced. We had each remarried, and all through the years my son had been adamant that he NEVER wanted to live with his father, so this decision came as a total surprise.

I asked him why, and I was not prepared for what I heard next. "Because you are a Christian and I can't stand being around you or your Christianity anymore!"

I felt as though I had been dealt a blow right to the heart and then knocked to my knees. The pain was excruciating, but there is strength when you are on your knees. God helped me to rise up, and make one of the hardest choices I've ever had to make. I told my son that I loved him very much, and that he was always welcome in our home, but that I could not and would not stop being who God had called me to be just because it made him uncomfortable. We both cried and hugged each other, and he moved out a week later.

Many nights after that I cried myself to sleep. I felt as though I had lost my son. My husband tried to reassure me that I hadn't lost him, he was just living in a different house but he was still my son. But the hurt was almost more than I could bear. I cried out to the Lord, "Lord, why? Why? Not my son. Please, please don't take my son! This costs too much! I don't think I can bear it. Please God, he's my only son!!

I felt the Lord say, "I know exactly how you feel." The realization set in as I wept, "Oh, forgive me Lord. I guess You do understand. This pain is so great. I can't even imagine how You felt, Lord. My sin cost You everything.... the very life of Your Son." Yes, this was painful, but now I knew He would see me through it. I felt strengthened somehow, knowing that He not only understood my pain, He had gone through far more than I could imagine.

I can't tell you that the next few days, months or years were easy. But, I can tell you that God gave me the courage to walk by faith during that difficult time. Our daughters were watching to see if Jesus really was first in my life, as I had proclaimed. I had talked the talk, and now, I had to walk the walk. The world is watching too. Watching to see how we, as Christians, handle our tribulations. Persevere, press on, God is always faithful. Over the next few years each of our daughters came to know Christ as their personal Savior. Hallelujah! And at age 18, my son asked to come home and stay with us for 6 weeks before going into the Navy. During his 4 years of service, he called and emailed many times, asking me to pray for someone he knew that was in need. I know that God has an amazing plan for my son's life, and I trust that one day, he will know that, too. My son and his wife live close to us now and we have a wonderful relationship.

James 1:12 says, "Blessed is a man who perseveres under trial; for once he has been approved, he will receive the crown of life which the Lord has promised to those who love Him.

Whatever trial, whatever tribulation, you may be going through right now, I want to encourage you to persevere and press on. For the Word says we should exult in our tribula-

72

tions, knowing that tribulation brings about perseverance, and perseverance, proven character, and proven character, hope.

Lord, Thank you that we can rejoice even in tribulation, knowing that You are producing godly character within us. Strengthen us to walk the walk of faith, no matter what the circumstances are, even though we can't see or know all You have planned for us. Comfort us in the knowledge of You, knowing that You work all things together for good for those that love You and are called according to Your purpose. We love you Lord. Help us to daily pick up our cross and follow You. In Jesus name, AMEN

"FORE"

Golf-now there's an interesting sport. My husband is a pretty good golfer. He also enjoys watching it on television. Now that is a bit beyond me. I can't even see the little ball until it finally lands, and I am always amazed at the crowd it draws to watch. It doesn't get much more boring than that in my book, unless, of course, you are watching a "fishing" show. I just don't understand where the suspense is. My husband will be intensely watching as I proclaim, "I can already tell you what is going to happen. He's going to catch a fish. They'll each look at it and say, "Nice fish". Then they'll let it go, and cast out again for another. Now do we have to watch it since you know the end of the story?" I can't get away with saying that for golf, because I really don't know how it will end. All I care about is WHEN it will end!

My husband decided that he would show me that golfing was fun by offering to teach me how to play. I was actually excited. I'd heard him and his buddies tell all of their golfing stories, so I was looking forward to this awesome bonding experience. We decided to go golfing with his brother and sister in law. What a great time this will be-just us 2 couples.

Now, I'm completely green when it comes to golfing. Hey, that was pretty good, green, golf, get it? The closest experience I have had to golfing was goofy golf, or as some call it, miniature golf. Which, I don't mind telling you, I consider myself pretty good at. So my confidence level was high in my preparation to get started.

My husband lovingly gave me instructions. Put the tee in the ground. Place the ball on the tee. Wrap your hands around the club, and interlock your fingers, with your thumb pointing down. This grip wasn't very comfortable. I don't know how they hit the ball like this. Oh yeah, keep your arm straight and bend one knee. What?? This was going to be harder than I had anticipated. I was contorted in some weird position as I "addressed" the ball. That's right, I said "addressed." I was learning the correct terminology as well. My husband was just a wealth of information. As I would swing, and completely miss the ball, I was informed that these "whiffs" counted as strokes against me because I had "addressed" the ball. In other words, I had meant to hit it, therefore it was not considered a practice swing. After accumulating approximately 25 of these whiffs, I was ready to address that ball all right, and it wasn't going to like what I had to say! My husband, in his infinite instructors' wisdom, said," Honey, HIT the ball," to which I immediately busted back with, "I'M TRYING!" But try as I might, the irritating little ball eluded me and my fingers were beginning to cramp from this position.

During my attempts a foursome had gathered behind us, patiently waiting for us to finish. My husband apologized to them for our taking so long, and explained it was my first time. They were very gracious and told us it was fine and that everyone had to learn sometime. However, after another 25 whiffs, they decided to take us up on the offer to play ahead. I guess they thought that I could continue learning after they were done. They all hit their balls, on their first attempts I might add, and off they went!

My husband instructed me to go ahead and "address" the ball again. This concerned me. I knew that in goofy golf, you must wait until the people in front of you have moved on to the next hole. My husband assured me that the people ahead of us were 150 yards away and were in no danger of being hit by my ball. He said I needn't be concerned, and to get on with my whiffing! So, I addressed the ball-this time with attitude, and WHACK! It landed within 2 feet of the people ahead of us. My husband hollered, "FORE!" They turned around to look, and when they saw it was me that hit the ball, they all cheered.

Now, it was my husband's turn. As he prepared to hit the ball, I thought this would be a good time to visit with my sister in law. I hadn't seen her in awhile. I began talking and was abruptly shushed! Apparently it is a faux pas to talk while someone else is hitting the ball. Oops-sorry! I waited, and when he had finished, I resumed my conversation. Now my brother in law was going to hit, and I was shushed again! I finally asked, "When do we get to talk?" From what I understand, all the conversation occurs while in the cart riding from stroke to stroke.

Everyone finished hitting, and we jumped in the carts. Off we went to our balls awaiting us in the fairway. My husband went to his, and instructed me to go to mine and do the "exact" same thing I had just done. So I did. The very first swing and "WHACK" again! My ball sailed through the air. My husband was impressed with my skill, and a bit proud of his incredible teaching ability. As we jumped in the cart and sped off, my hair blowing in the wind, I was thinking, hey this is fun! As I approached my ball again, I could see my husband watching out of the corner of his eye. He was so proud of his student, probably envisioning future circuit possibilities.

As I poked the tee in the ground, poised and ready to place my ball on it, I heard a yell. "WHAT ARE YOU DOING?"

"What do you mean, what am I doing? I'm doing what you told me to do." "YOU CAN'T USE A TEE IN THE FAIRWAY!!!"

"Why not? You told me to do the exact same thing I had done before, and that's exactly what I did!"

Apparently, the tees are only to be used the first time you hit the ball on a hole. The loss of the tee brought my golf career to a screeching halt! I never got to ride in the cart after that either, not because my husband wouldn't let me, but because my ball never traveled far enough to warrant getting in the cart. So much for bonding and talking.

As the day progressed, I grew more tired of all the walking and so much swinging. My arms were sore-where's the water? I was tired of golfing, and my husband was tired of me golfing. His patience had worn thin several holes ago, and he had given up trying to teach me. At the end of the game, as we all met in the parking lot-dehydrated, irritated and dragging, I announced, "I quit! Golf is NOT fun!! It's nothing like I expected, and I'm done!"

Sometimes we may feel that way about life. "I quit!" This is too hard! I'm sore, I'm tired, I'm thirsty, and I'm done! This isn't what I expected. I can't seem to get anywhere in this world. I try so hard, it's so much work, and I barely move forward. Do the cares of this world have you down to the point you've thought about giving up? Let me encourage you today-DON'T. Jesus can give you rest.

Jesus says in Matthew 11:28-30," Come to Me all who are weary and heavy laden and I will give you rest. Take My yoke upon you and learn from Me. I am gentle and humble in heart and you will find rest for your souls. For My yoke is easy and My burden is light." Let's give our burdens to the Lord today!

Lord, I'm so tired-tired of trying, and tired of striving. I've lost my passion for life, the very life which You've given me. Forgive me, Lord. As I lay these cares at Your feet, please pour afresh Your joy over me so that I will be strengthened with Your presence. Help me to rest in You, knowing I don't have to carry these burdens anymore. Thank You, Lord, for Your faithfulness and gentleness. In Jesus' name, Amen.

"No Pooh for You!"

Yard Sales-I love them. In someone else's yard. Actually I don't mind having them. It's the preparation in getting ready for them that I hate. Sorting, pricing, cleaning, lifting and sweating, especially in Arizona. Lots of sweating!

We have had enough yard sales by now that our children have realized that the work outweighs the fun. They were very young when we had our first yard sale, and were giddy with excitement. They diligently priced their items, and ambitiously sold hot dogs, too. They would jump for joy when someone would buy one of their items and soon they became caught up in the selling fever. It wasn't long before a crowd had gathered around them. I walked over to see what the big attraction was and was horrified to learn that they were selling their Barbie dolls and clothes, without my knowledge, for 10 cents a piece! They had gone in the house and were selling things I wasn't aware of! I could hear their groans of disappointment at lost sales as I quickly gathered up what was left of the Barbie items and rushed them inside. Although, now I think it may have actually been the customers I heard groaning when I made the discovery.

As the years have passed, our kids have become quite the bargainers. Now, you have to look hard to find something that's marked a dime. And if it's marked a dime-trust me-it's only worth a dime! Yard sales at our house get extremely hectic. Our home is in a great location, close to a major street. People seem to literally come out of the woodwork for our sales. They are everywhere. "Does this work? " "Can I plug this in?" "Where can I try this on?" "Will you take 50 cents for this?" "I'll give you $1.00 for all 3 items?" "My daughter needs to potty-can she use your bathroom?"

There are even shoplifters at yard sales. Oh Yes! They usually come in a group. One keeps you distracted asking a lot of questions and buying little nickel items, while another takes off with your nicer stuff. I guess we'll have to start attaching those magnetic sensors soon.

As you can tell, this is definitely more than a 2 person job! We learned the hard way not to advertise the sale in the newspaper, after wandering outside in the wee hours of the morning to start setting things out only to be greeted with customers. People have gone as far as to ring the doorbell the night before to see if we may have what they are looking for. Now, when we are ready, one of us goes and puts up signs, while the others prepare to work the crowd.

Since I have just set the stage for you, I want to tell you about one particular sale for the memory books. Our kids are grown now, with jobs of their own. Jobs that to them are far more important than our puny yard sales. Not to mention the fact that they make a lot more money at them too. My husband and I put the word out that we would be having a yard sale and if any of them wanted to sell anything they were welcome to. Everyone knows in our household that if you plan on sell-

80

ing then you better plan on helping, too. We've burned out the other children, but 2 of our daughters were still at home and vulnerable. Our youngest daughter had some things to sell, and assured us she would get her items priced. Our oldest daughter said she had some things, but we could sell them and keep the money. She wanted NO PART of the sale. She preferred her sleep.

The much anticipated morning came early...4:30 am. As my husband and I feverishly worked to move all the items out for the sale, I decided I better go awaken our youngest for help. She was exhausted. She had worked until 1am, and hadn't gotten to bed until 2. Oh the poor dear. She begged for a little extra sleep. Okay-but we were going to need some help soon, so I tiptoed upstairs to wake our oldest daughter. In my sweetest voice, I softly asked if she would come and help. I explained her sister's lack of rest, but she was not moved with compassion. She moaned, and reminded me that she had already said we could keep the money. That's true I thought, she shouldn't have to help-okay, I'll let her sleep.

Soon, my husband was ready to put the signs up, and there was no way I would be able to handle this crowd alone-nor would I be able to leave, once it started, in order to ask anyone for help again. It was time to get serious. I woke our youngest again with a desperate plea for help. She was furious. She didn't consider the extra 15 minutes as added sleep. An argument ensued and wound up with a demand that she get up NOW! As my snarling little entourage and I went out to start the sale, she asked where the price tags were and informed me that she was now planning on pricing her items! What-she didn't have that done? We couldn't afford to have her pricing items, we needed her for the sale!

I knew now there was no getting around it. I didn't want to ask, but at this point we were going to need all hands on deck. I crept back upstairs and said, "Doni, I know you're not interested in helping, but that's no longer the issue. We really need you. We can't do it alone."

All of a sudden, someone I didn't recognize as my daughter, sat up in her bed-hair sticking on end, and poking out all over. I think the head even twisted completely around, and growled, "I SAID, I DON'T WANT ANY PART OF THIS SALE!!"

Oh boy, never mind I thought. We'll figure it out. I don't want a demon at the yard sale! So I told her to forget it, but by now it had crawled out of bed, and was screaming, "I'M UP NOW!'

I told her to go back to bed, but she yelled, "OH NO-I AM HELPING!!!" Are we going to have fun today-yippee!! As we headed outside, I caught a glimpse in the mirror of Jillian, putting on her makeup, instead of pricing. This is unbeliev-able!!! We don't have time for makeup, I told her! Get outside! Finally, we were all present and accounted for. Let the games begin! No one was around and you can imagine how well that went over! Just then a big spender approached, or so we thought. It was a lady that picked up a stuffed Winnie the Pooh of Jillian's. It was in excellent condition. She asked how much, even though it was clearly marked $3.00. She wondered if I would take less for it, and I turned to the girls. Doni explained that my daughter had paid $27.00 for it at Disneyland, and it had never been played with, so she felt that $3.00 was a good price. Then the lady made a bold move, yet not bright, consid-ering the mood they were in, but how could she know? She offered $1.00 for it. Oh Lord, have mercy on her, she knows not what she does.

Her offer was quickly rejected, with a blunt clenched teeth answer, straight from Jillian, "I SAID $3.00!" From that point on, she became known to us as the "Pooh Lady." She car-ried that Pooh around the sale for quite sometime as she gath-ered up an armful of 5, 10, and 3 for 25 cents items. Finally,

Pooh Lady was ready to pay. She laid down all of her treasures except for Pooh, of course, and I cut off each price tag, and began to add them up. Her grand total with the Pooh, was $5.35.

"Oh I can't spend that much!" she said. So she decided to put some items back. Wonderful, all the price tags were off- I didn't know what went with what. What a mess! I diligently worked to separate all the items, and finally whittled her purchase down to $3.65. That included Pooh, but at this point, I wasn't sure if she still wanted it. She hadn't laid it in the keep pile. She was still holding it.

So I asked her, so I could be sure. She curtly replied," Of course I want it!" She gave a look and roll of the eyes, as if to say I was incompetent. After all of that, she then paid with a twenty and I gladly bagged up her purchases, thanked her and sent her on her way. Just in time, too, because my daughter's patience had worn thin and she was ready to yell, "NO POOH FOR YOU!!"

Before the day was over, we were laughing about the experience including their attitudes that morning.

Later, my daughter said, "Mom, I can't believe you were so nice to the Pooh Lady. You just kept smiling even after all she put you through and the way she treated you."

The way SHE treated me? Now that's funny! I've thought about that and I know it wasn't in my own strength, to smile and be nice to Pooh Lady. Believe me, my flesh was saying, "No Pooh for you!"

It was the character of Christ shining through me. The Bible says in *Romans 12:17-18*, *"Never pay back evil for evil to anyone. Respect what is right in the sight of all men. If possible, so far as it depends on you, be at peace with all men."* As far as it depends upon you, think about that. People are watching us to see if what we have makes a difference in our life. We may be telling them with our lips that they need Jesus, and yet our life may reflect a totally different story. Someone once said that you may be the only Bible someone reads. Ask yourself-what does my life say to those around me?

Galatians 6:9 says *Let us not lose heart in doing good, for in due time we will reap if we do not grow weary.*

Father, Oh how I long to be like You. I know I fail many times to show Your love to others. I sometimes lose my temper. Forgive me, Lord. Help me to be patient with others, to be able to forgive just as You have forgiven me. May my life reflect Your glory to those around me, knowing it is not me, but Christ in me. Be magnified in my life this day, and always. In Jesus' name AMEN.

"Can You Pass a White Glove Inspection?"

In the years of my growing up, cleaning was a major part of our daily lives. My parents were fanatics about it. At least, that's how I viewed them. My Dad had been in the Marines, and I think he always wanted to be a Drill Sergeant - so you get the picture? One of the things, that brought him great delight, was to periodically hold, "white glove inspections." Now granted, he didn't actually put on a white glove, he just called it that. He would run his finger along different pieces of furniture, or whatever he chose to inspect, looking for dirt while we would hold our breath in nervous anticipation. When he found dirt, and he always seemed to find some, he would proclaim, "AH HAH!" That's when we knew we would have to clean some more. Needless to say, we cleaned a lot!

One time in particular, when I was in high school, I had been invited to go somewhere with my friends. I came to my Dad and asked if I could go. He asked, "Is your room clean?" I replied, "Yes." He said, "Can it pass a white glove inspection?"

Uh oh--- "Just a minute" I said. I went to my room to double check and carefully make sure that I hadn't missed anything. I knew he always somehow found dirt, but this time, I had worked extra hard and I was sure I had gotten it all. It was perfect, so I went back and confidently announced, my room could pass, and the inspection began.

My Dad turned to me before starting, and stated, "Now, if I find anything -you're not going." So he began to run his finger along the furniture, the top of the doorway, the baseboards, hoping to find some dirt. He was poised, and ready to claim, "AH HAH" at any given moment of discovery, but each time he found none. I was getting excited, and grew more confident. "Dad, please, can I go?" "Just a minute", he would say, as he ran his finger along the electrical switch plates on the walls. I smiled as his finger, again, revealed no dirt. He checked the hinges on the door, as well as the light bulb in the lamp, still, no dirt. "Come on Dad please?" But he didn't respond, as he opened my closet, and proceeded to wipe along the shelf. Once again-no dirt! Now I will admit, by now I was becoming frustrated, and a little cocky. I whined, "Dad please, you're not going to find anything. I got it all. It's spotless! Can I go now?" This time, very slowly and thoughtfully, he replied, "Just a minute." Now by thoughtful, I mean I could tell he was thinking about where to check next, and I watched in disbelief, as he got out a screwdriver, and began to remove the back from my clock radio. You have got to be kidding. He then ran his finger along the electrical components and gleefully exclaimed, "AH HAH!!"

This was more than I could take and I began to cry. "Dad that's not fair!!"

He looked long and hard at me, and then proudly informed me with this. "I'm going to go ahead and let you go, THIS TIME, BUT just remember, that no matter how hard you try, or how good you do, you will NEVER EVER beat me!"

I was glad to get to go, and yet I was crushed at the same time. I will never forget that. I felt defeated. I had spent many years trying to be good enough, but it was never enough. Maybe you've felt defeated too? Have you spent your life striving to be perfect and yet never measuring up? Have you pictured God sitting up in heaven waiting to ask, "Can you pass a white glove inspection?"

Well there will be an inspection, it's called "Judgment Day" You can spend all your time cleaning, to prepare for it, but there is only one way to pass it. You can't pass it on your own, none of us can. The Bible says in *Romans 3:10, "There is none righteous, not one."* No matter how clean you try to make yourself, how good you think you are, God will always find dirt! It's Christ's righteousness, not ours. The Bible says that our righteousness is as filthy rags. We must repent of our sin, ask for forgiveness and put on the Lord Jesus Christ.

Psalm 51:6 Behold You desire truth in the inward parts, And in the hidden part You will make me to know wisdom. Just like my Dad looked at the inward parts of my clock radio and found dirt, so too God will look at our inward parts, every thought, word, and deed, and He will find dirt! There is no hope to pass inspection except through the blood of Jesus Christ! When we are in Christ, we are righteous in God's sight. Then, and only then can we pass inspection.

Lord please forgive me for thinking I could be good enough to pass Your inspection. I realize now that I am filthy dirty. I'm so sorry and I want to repent of my sin today. Please cleanse me from all unrighteousness. Thank You for the gift of salvation. I don't deserve it and I know now I can't earn it. I can't fathom that kind of love, that would sacrifice Your own Son for me, and I am forever grateful. I want to live the rest of my life glorifying You.

In Jesus' name, AMEN.

"How Will You be Found?"

When I was a child, my parents both worked out of the home. That meant that during the summer, my 2 sisters and I would be home alone all day. My Dad was the first one to arrive home at the end of the day because His shift started very early in the morning. My Mom would leave us a list of work that was to be done BEFORE we did anything else, i.e. play, or watch TV. Most of the time, the list seemed impossible to finish. We would divide up the jobs, so that each of us had our own part to do. And if we all worked together, we could get done. But if any one of us didn't do our part, the work didn't get finished. Many times we would start fighting, and then beating on each other, and when that happened, forget it-there was no way we were going to get it done!

One day in particular, we looked at the list and it seemed unusually easy, so we felt confident we had plenty of time to get everything finished. After all, we had all day. We all agreed that we would watch a couple of our favorite TV programs FIRST, and then, if we all worked really hard, we would still get done and no one would be the wiser! We were going to get the work done and be able to enjoy ourselves, so how could this hurt anything? So we turned on the TV, and it wasn't long before we became entranced with our favorite programs and we would say, just one more. There were so many good shows, one right after the other! Suddenly, we heard a car door, and we were horrified to discover that Dad was home earlier than expected! We jumped up, turned off the TV, and quickly began working. But, when Dad came in the door, He wasn't fooled. He knew we hadn't been doing the work we were supposed to do. In fact, he walked right over to the TV, and felt the back of it, and, of course, it was warm. BUSTED!!!!

The Bible says in Matthew 24:43-51;"But know this, that if the master of the house had known what hour the thief would come, he would have watched and not allowed his house to be broken into." Therefore you also be ready, for the Son of Man is coming at an hour you do not expect. "Who then is a faithful and wise servant, whom his master made ruler over his household, to give them food in due season? " Blessed is that servant whom his master, when he comes, will find so doing. "Assuredly, I say to you that he will make him ruler over all his goods. "But if that evil servant says in his heart, 'My master is delaying his coming,' "and begins to beat his fellow servants, and to eat and drink with the drunkards, "the master of that servant will come on a day when he is not looking for him and at an hour that he is not aware of, "and will cut him in two and appoint him his portion with the hypocrites. There shall be weeping and gnashing of teeth.

As I was studying this scripture, I was thinking about the story of my sisters and I, and I believe the Lord gave me this analogy about the Body of Christ. He has given us a job to do. He has promised He is coming back for His church, but in the meantime, we are to be busy doing what He has commanded. He said, *"Go, into all the world and preach the gospel to every creature."* (Mark 16:15)

We the church, have allowed the worldly cares and desires to distract us from what our Father has commanded. Many of us are spending our time arguing and bickering amongst ourselves over petty differences. We have even beaten each other up-our fellow servants in the kingdom. And we haven't paid attention that all the while the thief is robbing us! He is robbing us of the harvest. He is robbing us of our witness. It has been severely compromised because the world views us and sees that we can't even get along amongst ourselves! Instead of working together, we are fighting each other. Therefore our testimony is tainted and we aren't the salt and light that God has called us to be! And we wonder why the world is so lost and desolate? We are in this battle together. We need to work together to win the lost and bring the light of Christ to this darkened world!

Jesus is coming back at an hour that we do not know! We must be ready! Each one of us has a job to do. So, now, let me ask. What about you personally? Are you doing what the Lord has commanded you to do? Or have you let the worries and attractions of this world distract you from the very thing God has called you to do? We will all give an account one day for how we have spent what was given to us. Let's be about our Father's business.

Lord,

Forgive us. We have not sought You with our whole heart. If we had, this world-would be transformed. We repent for our complacency. Father, forgive us, and burn a passion in our hearts to seek and save the lost-to proclaim the day of Your coming, and the triumphant victory in You! In Jesus' name we pray, AMEN.

Just the Way He Wants Me

Before becoming a Christian, I let the world and those around me determine my self worth. I didn't realize who I was in Christ, because I wasn't "in" Christ. Therefore, my self worth was wrapped up in how I looked and what other people thought of me. Can anyone relate?

We can be so critical of ourselves. I have always used a lot of humor, and cut myself down before anyone else could, thereby thinking if anyone made fun of me, I'd beat them to it, and somehow, it would hurt less. Remember that old saying, "Sticks and stones may break my bones, but words will never hurt me?" NOT TRUE!

Growing up, I always made jokes that my sisters took after our mom in the chest department, and I took after my dad. That's right-a nickname I was given in Jr. High was "Flatsy" I really was flat, there's no denying that! I could put on 2 snoopy Band-Aids and have a "designer bra." I think when I was in line for breasts, God dropped my portion on the ground, and it bounced up and attached to my ankles. Really, my ankles are so thick, if I want to wear an ankle bracelet I have to buy a choker! Anyway, I was always keenly aware that I was lacking in the breast department.

My wonderful husband of one year, thought that since I made jokes about how small I was, that he could too! And he somehow thought that I would find them funny. Now we all know that was not the case. I didn't find them, or him, funny at all.

One of his particular attempts at breast humor was none other than on Christmas Eve. Christmas is always a wonderful time of gathering together and we happened to be at some friends' house that evening. There were a lot of people there and we had just arrived. I was wearing my new Christmas sweater. It was beautiful. It was red with streamers all down the front and jingle bells on the end of each of one. Someone said to me," Sherry, shake your jingle bells."

As I started to shimmy, my encouraging husband said, "Are you kidding? She doesn't have anything to shake the bells with!"

I graciously chuckled and said, "That's true," all the while thinking to myself that better be the last crack from my little newly wed. Now in the room amongst our friends was one friend in particular, Arnold. He's what I call a little guy, muscular, but very short for a man. Of course, I'm 6ft tall, so almost everyone seems small to me.

Anyway, as I was definitely anxious to move past the subject of my chest, another zinger rolls off my husband's lips. "Arnold's pecks are bigger than Sherry's."

OH NO, he did not just say that! Smile. Keep your composure. Don't cry. Everyone was looking at me. You know, with that look of pity, when you feel sorry for someone and you really don't know what to say? There was silence in the room. No one laughed. No one except for my precious comedian, who had just cracked himself up with what he thought was a hysterical joke! I maintained my composure, but needless to say, Santa was in trouble!

I waited until we got into the car to express my feelings. Let me just say, that after much discussion, a few months, and $ 5,000 later, I had breastsis!

I remember waking up from surgery with my new silicone implants. All I remember thinking was how heavy these things were! You mean I'm going to have to carry these things around forever? My chest weighs a ton! They'll break my back. I had never thought about them being heavy. Good thing I have these thick ankles for support!

As months progressed, it was like my body realized I had more on top, so it needed to pad the other areas to help balance me out. Men started staring at my chest instead of talking to me, and the clothes that used to fit so cute, now made me feel like a cow! To make matters worse, when you have implants, they have to do extra long mammograms. Yippee!! Now that's a treat!

Well, I got what I wanted, but at what cost? Isn't it funny the things we will do for approval from society or those around us to feel as though we have worth? We do have worth, no matter what we look like or how others see us. You see, God created me just the way He wants me, and He has created

Father, Help me to see that I am precious in Your sight. Renew my mind, and help me to stop being critical of how You have created me. Help me to stay focused on You when others say hurtful things. Give me a spirit of forgiveness towards them, for they know not what they do. Please heal any past hurts that I may be harboring, and cleanse my mind of negative thoughts about myself. Help me to see myself and others as You do. May I see through love covered lenses. In Jesus' name, Amen you just the way He wants you, too. You are beautiful to Him. He is your author and His work is good! You're a daughter of the King, and you are loved. You are loved so much that He gave His only Son for you. Before you were born, He knit you in your mother's womb. Don't let anyone or anything tell you differently. You are loved by God, and you are precious in His sight. Let's ask God to renew our minds so that we can understand His incredible love for us.

"Look Out For the Tongue!"

James 3:8 "But no one can tame the tongue; it is a restless evil and full of deadly poison."

THEN WHAT IS IT DOING IN MY SANDWICH?? Out of the blue, with no warning, never saw it coming, I opened my Man from U.N.C.L.E. lunch box and wham!!! A tongue sandwich! You can imagine my horror. That is pretty scary stuff for a little kid.

Granted, it was Beef Tongue-SO WHAT!!! To a second grader, it looked like my own lying between 2 pieces of bread. It even had the bumps on it! I have since learned that you are supposed to skin those off, but my Mother didn't know that at the time. Now, that is one task I REFUSE to experience.

What's worse is-how do you trade this? How am I going to pass this off? I will admit I was a picky eater-but beef tongue-let's be real. I hated "Braunswauger" too, but it was looking mighty good that day!!

Now it was lunchtime. "Let's make a deal."

But after repeated attempts to trade, the scenario was always the same... "Hey, I'll trade you sandwiches."

"What do you have?"

"Umm...Beef-what do you have?"

" Peanut Butter and Jelly". As I would begin to lick my lips, the dreaded question would come up. "What's your beef look like? Let me see it." I would gingerly open the bread to reveal IT. Their eyes would grow as big as saucers, as they jumped back 3 feet and exclaimed, "WHOA-WHAT IS THAT?" My sentiments exactly!

I would try to act nonchalant, as I would say, "Beef Tongue."

"NO WAY-I'M NOT TRADING!"

As time passed, it became very apparent that I was going to remain hungry that day. After several attempts, not only had I failed at trading the tongue, but by now talk had spread throughout the lunchroom and kids were all coming over just to see the specimen, not trade for it. I had my own little show and tell going on. I couldn't even get anyone to take it to the trash for me. We were all afraid to touch it.

When it came time to leave, I carefully pulled up on the sides of the plastic wrap, so as to avoid it touching me. Then I gently lifted it out and hurled it into the trash can. Free, at last! Imagine my surprise when I got home and discovered jars of the "pickled poison" sitting on the counter. When will this nightmare end???

If only we would be that careful in handling our own tongues. How many times have thoughtless remarks rolled off of our tongues like poison and contaminated those around us.

Just like the tongue in my sandwich caused talk to spread throughout the lunchroom, so our own tongues have spread talk about others throughout our lives. Oh the tongue-that we would learn to control it!

Proverbs 18:21" Death and life are in the power of the tongue and those who love it will eat it's fruit."

I didn't eat it then and I'm not eating it now!!! Let's use our tongues to speak life, not death.

Lord,

I come to You today with sorrow in my heart, sorrow for all of the times that I have chosen to speak words that hurt, instead of heal. Forgive me Lord, and help me to bridle my tongue. Help me, to speak words of encouragement, to those around me. Help me, to refrain from gossip, and have nothing to do with it. May I always speak kindly of others. Change my heart, Oh God, because You say, out of the abundance of the heart, the mouth speaks. Help my heart, to be so abundant with Your love that it pours from my mouth. Thank You Lord, for Your mercy, that is new every morning. In Jesus' name, AMEN.

What Matters Most

I was in the middle of a craft project, when the frantic call came to "come quickly!" My 14yr. old daughter, Doni, had been hit in the head at volleyball practice and would need stitches. As I quickly gathered a small bag of ice, I thought, "Hit in the head? At volleyball? Volleyball isn't dangerous." I envisioned the ball must have hit her in her mouth with her braces.

When I got to the school to pick her up, she was sitting down holding an icepack to her forehead. The coach explained that my daughter had been assisting in taking down the net, and the crank that pulls the net taut was old and had stuck. When it did finally release, it flew back and hit her in the forehead. She never lost consciousness, but the injury was deep and she would definitely need stitches. I later found out that the velocity in which the crank struck her was approx. 100 mph!

I drove her to the hospital, and I kept her talking all the

way there. After I explained the situation, a nurse looked at her injury and then offered us a seat in the waiting room. They'd be with us shortly. Thirty minutes later her ice pack was warm, so I ran out to the van to get the other ice I had brought.

I was only gone seconds, and when I came back, my daughter gave me this funny look. Her eyes grew quite large and she wasn't responding to my questions. She started flipping her insurance card on her leg back and forth, back and forth. I called for the nurse and they immediately ushered her back, while I was informed that they were ready to do my paperwork now.

PAPERWORK? Something is drastically wrong with my daughter, and now they're ready to do paperwork and they expect me to know information? I couldn't even remember my own phone number at this point! My husband was out of town. I could barely remember my name. But God is faithful and the only number I could remember was my Pastor's, so I called and left a message.

My son and his dad arrived just as the nurse announced I could see her. I had called him on our way to the hospital. I quickly went in. Nothing could have prepared me for what was about to happen. There was my daughter sitting on the bed, looking up at the ceiling and rocking back and forth.

When I inquired as to why she was doing that, the nurse said, "She didn't know," and then immediately left the area!

As I touched my daughter, saying her name to let her know I was there, she suddenly started growling, curled up in a ball, and wet all over herself. She was in a seizure!

Shouts rang out," We definitely have a fractured skull, possible brain damage! We need a CAT scan immediately!"

As they stabbed her with an anti-seizure medication, I felt my faith spirally downward. I was watching my precious daughter fighting for her life, and there was nothing I could do. Words cannot explain how helpless I felt! If only I could get close enough to touch my baby, and pray for her. But she was whisked away for a CAT scan. Even now, tears are filling my eyes, as I try to describe the emotion I was feeling.

They led us to a special waiting area while she was having the scan done. I put my head down, and began to sob and pray. I know I prayed harder than I had ever done in my life! I was begging the Lord to please save my little girl! It seemed like an eternity. And to be honest, I have no idea how much time passed. But I can tell you that God flooded me with such a peace. I know now what peace that passes understanding means. I heard His voice assuring me that even though this was a terrible thing, He was going to make it right. She would be fine. I dried my eyes, and told my son and his dad that the Lord said she was going to be alright.

Now you must know this, my children's father and I were in a tense situation. We were in the middle of a 2 year bitter court battle with each other, both of us determined to win. We hadn't been able to speak to each other civilly in quite a while.

When we were finally able to see Doni, relief poured over us! She was actually talking and knew who we were. But the journey was just beginning. She did have a skull fracture, and would need to be transported by helicopter to a nearby neurological hospital for surgery. Meanwhile, the waiting room out front had filled with friends and family praying for Doni. What a comfort that was.

All night we sat with her in the intensive care unit, her dad and I. In the morning she would be having surgery, but as we watched our beautiful daughter sleep, we were overcome with gratefulness that we still had her with us. We began to realize how ridiculous it was to hold this grudge against each other. We were realizing what matters most. We almost lost our child. Our petty differences were just that-petty-and it was time to let go of them.

Morning came and my husband arrived just in time for her surgery. The doctors didn't know the extent of the damage. They would know more once they got in there. They explained the procedure, and surgery was soon underway. There were so many people there praying with us, and for us. The hospital had to install a private phone line in the ICU room so that we could help field some of the calls coming in from everywhere. News had spread fast, and everyone was anxious to hear how she was doing.

When the operation was finally over, the surgeon came out to speak with us. They had cut her head from ear to ear, and peeled down her forehead. Bone was then harvested from the back of her skull to help repair the damage. A titanium plate with screws was secured into her forehead area. They closed it all with approximately 200 stitches underneath, and 80 staples holding her head together, all without shaving her head! Amazing!

After explaining, the neurosurgeon said this," In an injury like this, it is always a given that there is a hole in the dura, the lining of the brain. Not only was there not a hole, the dura hadn't even been touched!"

There is no doubt in my mind that God did just what He said He would do---a miracle! As Doni recuperated in the hospital, I stayed those 5 days with her and we ate, and colored, and played games. It was a wonderful time of bonding with my daughter that I will never forget. Even as I write this story, I can't help but weep with gratitude for God's grace and mercy, and how He carried us through.

His grace and mercy have carried us through many

101

experiences in life, and I am continually in awe of Him. *Romans 8:28 And we know that all things work together for good to those who love God, to those who are called according to His purpose.* Even though, some may say it's hard to see the good in this, I certainly can. God used it to mend relationships and increase our faith. My daughter became very aware of who God is, and our faith was a witness to friends, family, and hospital employees.

I'm sorry that it took something like this for me to learn such a valuable lesson. Jesus lives in me, and He empowers me to rise above petty differences and walk with integrity. He's called me to a higher place. When we as Christians bicker, argue, and hold grudges, we are acting like the world. Jesus is not better known and loved by our actions. We must always remember who we are and Whose we are. Our lives and attitudes should reflect the character of Christ.

Isaiah 40:31But those who wait on the Lord shall renew their strength; They shall mount up with wings like eagles, They shall run and not be weary, They shall walk and not faint.

Father,

Forgive me for my petty differences, whether I am right is not the issue. Forgiveness is what You have given and forgiveness is what You require. Help me to keep the main thing, the main thing-my relationship with You, with a pure desire to know You and make You known. May my life always reflect Your grace and mercy that You have so lavished on me. Help me to mount up with wings like eagles and rise above my circumstances. Thank You Lord, for saving my soul, and for saving my daughter. In Jesus' name, AMEN

Plastic Perfection

When I was growing up, we had a room in our house called "the good living room". Maybe you had one of these? A special room only for company-NO ONE ELSE ALLOWED! There was only one catch! It was adjacent to the front door. You had to walk through it in order to get to the other rooms in the house. This created a problem.

Mom and Dad were extremely regimented in the cleaning department. The room had to look perfect! So a plastic runner was placed from the entryway through the "good living room" to the family room. You were allowed to walk only on the plastic runner. This was to allow for the traffic flow without dirtying the carpet. The only time we could walk on the carpet in the good living room was on cleaning days.

The scenario was always the same, roll back the runner, scrub the mopboards and windowsills, dust the furniture, water the plant, and end with vacuuming straight lines in the carpet. They must be perfect. Every line should meet without overlapping. Then roll back the runner, and Voila! PERFEC-TION! There was a white brocade couch for the guests with a clear plastic cover in order to keep it looking fresh and new. That way, you could see the beautiful brocade but avoid soiling it when you sat on it.

Doesn't the sound of this room just sort of agitate you? Well it did my sisters and me. We were tired of always cleaning that room, and for what? We called it the "rubber room". However, "plastic parlor" seems more apropos. I don't even remember anyone ever sitting in there. I mean, how comfortable can you be sitting on a sofa with a plastic cover on it? Sounds so inviting doesn't it? Now you know how kids are? When you tell them they shouldn't do something-that's the exact thing they want to do! And we were no different.

So one night, our parents were going out and we had a sitter. I was about 10 years old at the time and my sisters were 12 and 8. The baby sitter asked us what we wanted to do that would be fun, and we could all enjoy. We decided we wanted to dance, and the rubber room would be a perfect venue for it! So we rolled back the runner, whipped off the plastic cover from the white brocade couch. After all, you must admit, plastic is not very conducive for dancing. We moved some of the furniture, and put on "Gold Finger," the elusive album that we had been instructed was only for adults.

We took turns dancing on the couch, doing gymnastics across the carpeting, all without the runner. We were having a blast! Our boldness created an excitement in the air. We were rebels and we knew it! It was very important that no one else did, however! We knew we didn't dare continue our fun for long, because who knew how long Mom and Dad would be gone? We couldn't take a chance in getting caught.

So, after our "risky business," we moved the furniture back, replaced the plastic cover on the couch, carefully vacuumed the straight lines back in the carpet, and then rolled out the plastic runner. They never knew.

We finally told our mother 30 years later. We still haven't told Dad. I think we'll wait on that one. Oops--Dad, if you're reading this-sorry.

We can spend our whole life striving for perfection, and we'll never get it! We must humble ourselves and seek forgiveness for our sin against God and our arrogance in thinking we could be good enough. We must put on the Lord Jesus Christ and invite Him into our home completely, not direct Him to stay on the plastic runner, in the good living room. We must risk letting Him know that things aren't perfect. He already knows that anyway. And guess what? Once we invite Him in, He'll help us clean the whole house, not just the areas people see. It's a process, and it takes time, but He promises to finish the good work He has started in us.

Lord, I'm tired of striving for perfection. I can't do it, I need You! You are the only thing perfect. Please forgive my sins, and my arrogant attitude of thinking I could do it on my own. Wash away all the cobwebs and dirt that have built up in the recesses of my heart. Remodel, remold, and reconstruct any areas that are not pleasing in Your sight. Thank You, that my heart is now Your home, and I am no longer in charge or alone. In Jesus' name, Amen.

From Messed Up to Dressed Up!

Weddings can be emotional times, especially when it's your own child getting married. We experienced a double dose this year. Our oldest daughter Doni got married, and a short 4 months later, our youngest daughter Jillian did also, leaving us with an empty nest!

Jillian's wedding was set to be in the mountains, in the cool air amidst the oak and pine trees. We were all renting cabins and it was going to be a great trip. Two days before we were to leave for the wedding, I knocked over a marble and brass lamp, which landed directly on my toe. It started swelling immediately and eventually caused my whole foot to swell up, not to mention the lovely shades of purple I was sporting! How attractive for the mother of the bride, but I soon found out the bruises were the least of my concern. I couldn't walk on my foot properly, so I ended up hobbling around by walking on the inside of my foot. Needless to say, it slowed me down considerably, not to mention, caused great pain. Plus it added a long trip to the mall to get new shoes that would now accommodate my Barney Rubble foot.

When we arrived a day later to our cabins, last minute preparations still needed to be done. Swollen or not, I was determined to do my part. The morning of the wedding, bright and early at 7am, we left to decorate the little country church where the ceremony was to be. My husband was not going along to help decorate as that's not one of his fortes. So before leaving, I made one request of him. Please get the sound machine out of the trunk of the car while I am gone and bring it into the cabin. I still had a couple of recordings to do for the ceremony that afternoon and pictures were at noon. With my foot the way it was, the machine was too big and bulky for me to maneuver myself. He assured me he would take care of it!

We finished all the decorating and, I must say, it looked beautiful. I could just picture my gorgeous daughter walking down through the trees in her wedding dress. This would be a day to remember! I was looking forward to spending time with her as she dressed for her wedding. I was careful with my walking and was actually doing quite well. When I got back to our cabin, I intended to quickly get the sound done, and then go over and help Jillian get ready.

As I walked in the cabin, guess what I found? Nothing-no sound machine and no husband! Now I had attitude! I was thinking-I give him one job-ONE JOB-and he can't even do that! Oh I know, you've never felt that way. Well I'm sorry, I did! And of course along with this attitude came the illusion of being invincible. Fine, I'll get it out myself, hurt foot or not. I guess if you want something done right, you have to do it yourself! Wait till he shows up, that man will be getting an earful! Muttering to myself, I made my way to the trunk of the car, but I wasn't paying close enough attention to where I was walking. The slipper I was wearing caught on a railroad tie in the ground. As I began to lose my balance, and was about to fall, I quickly caught myself on my already injured foot-OUCH! That did it! Now it hurt to walk at all, and my tears began to fall. My daughter-in-law had just come out of their cabin next door and offered to help me. As she unloaded the sound machine, I stayed by my baby granddaughter. She kept wrinkling up her face and pointing to my foot and saying, "owie?" Yeah Grammy has an owie alright-but Papa will be the next one with one.

When the machine was all in place, my daughter-in-law helped me inside, and then left for her walk. As I sat there, tears streaming down my face from the pain, I began to wonder what, if anything, I would be able to participate in now. I decided I better try to elevate my throbbing foot. I had just done that when my daughter and her mother-in-law-to-be arrived. They were so thoughtful, and had brought me some of the rolls from the free continental breakfast, so this mangled martyr explained her story to them. As I gushed out what happened, they were so concerned and sent for ice to put on my foot. My daughter asked, "Do you think its okay for you to be alone?" I assured her that I wasn't suicidal, and I explained that I would just keep my foot up with the ice and enjoy my rolls and work on the music-not to worry. They left and hence my quiet time began.

When I finished up the music, thoughts came flooding in reminding me that at my other daughter's wedding, I was actually with her as she got ready. I so wished I could see Jillian getting ready right then. I should be with her! This was my last time to really be alone with her and enjoy her as my single little girl. I couldn't watch her get ready and I couldn't even walk over and ask her to get ready over at my cabin. I couldn't call her, because there were no phones and no signal for our cell phones either! At this point I realized that I would be the only one coming to my pity party! I decided I might as well play some music, so I put in a CD and a song came on from my oldest daughter's wedding and it was all over-I was a mess, bawling like a baby and my party was now in full swing!

Then my daughter-in-law stopped by to check on me, and I wailed about the sadness I was feeling and the special moments I was missing that a mother looks forward to. She was so gracious to listen and sympathize with me. Then my mother and mother-in-law came in-they were sharing our cabin. They took one look at me and my mother said, "I wondered how long it would take before it would hit you?" That got me going so I went through the whole story again. As my husband came through the door he was surprised to find us all there and me in such a state. You would have been so proud of me---I calmly explained what happened...that I had been injured while trying to get the sound machine out of the trunk, and I paused for the apology. None came, he said, 'I told you that I'd get that out, why didn't you wait for me?" Apparently he had not heard me say I wanted it done before I got back. Meanwhile he had gone fishing at the creek with our grandsons. As I went on with my story and the loss I was feeling and what I was missing out on, my husband, in his compassionate wisdom, said, "Oh knock it off and get off it!" I'm not sure that's what I needed to hear, and I know it's not what I wanted to hear, but it was effective and the pity party was over. The wedding was beautiful and it was a wonderful day, despite my mourning.

How many times have we wallowed in self pity and focused more on our circumstances than on the God over our circumstances? *Matthew 6:33 Seek first the kingdom of God and His righteousness and all these other things shall be added unto you.* We have God's promises-if we seek Him and His righteousness first-He'll give us everything we need, including the strength to see beyond our circumstances and trust God in the midst of them. You know it's funny how one little part of the body, like a toe, can cause the whole body to suffer. And it's like that in the Body of Christ, too. When we get our focus off of the One we are to be living for, and on to our own little per-

109

sonal agendas-the whole Body suffers. Each of us is called for Kingdom purposes. God has a job for us to do-to seek and save the lost, and when we let the aches and pains of our own lives change our focus, the whole Body is affected.

Lord,

I want to function according to Your standards and not my own. Help me to seek and save the lost as You have called me to do. May I work in unity with You for the sake of the call and keep my eyes focused on You, the Head, and not on the tale of my circumstances. Help me not to dwell on how big my circumstances are, but to remember how big my God is! In Jesus' name, AMEN

It's Good For You

I grew up a very finicky eater, but as the years pass, I am hard pressed to find a food I don't like. One thing I do hate, and have always hated, is fat. I can't stand to eat it. I don't like it on my body, on my plate, and especially not on my meat! If even a small piece gets in my mouth I start gagging, and trust me, it's not a pretty sight. I know, I know, I've been told that fat makes the meat more tender. But as a child, I didn't care. I wondered why they didn't just make the meat without it.

My mom loved fat, and always chimed that it was the best part. Yuck! She could have had mine, but I guess she didn't want to deprive me of it-oh goodie! Now I do have to give my parents credit. They tried to cut most of it off for me, but somehow I always managed to get some. So I had to devise a clever scheme for getting rid of it. Now this was easier said than done. The rule was you must eat everything on your plate-even if it took all night. I soon learned there was no point in trying to out wait my parents. Tomorrow would be a new day, with fresh opportunities to finish my lovely leftovers. So, I had to comprise a new plan. We had a dog, but she wasn't allowed in the house, so she wouldn't be any help. I tried everything I could think of. First, I went with the whole napkin thing-casually stowing the nasty hunks within the paper, and nonchalantly throwing it away. That didn't work. It was quite noticeable that my hands were smaller than the wad I was carrying, and my parents were no dummies. Then I struck the toilet idea! I poked meat in my mouth and asked to be excused to the bathroom, where I would spit it all out and flush. The problem was that I could only take small amounts at a time, otherwise it would be too obvious that the meat was gone too quickly, not to mention talking with those puffy cheeks. And, the frequent trips to the bathroom raised suspicion and it wasn't long before that plan was foiled.

Finally, out of desperation, I stumbled onto something that worked. I would place the meat into my mouth and chew, and chew, and chew, and when no one was looking, quickly take it out and carefully tuck it under the edge of my plate. With each piece, I would methodically go through the motions. When I was finished, my parents were so proud, and so was I. I had finally conceived of and carried out a plan that worked! The key in the success of all of this was to make sure when cleaning up that I grabbed my plate before someone else did. That way, I could quickly scoop up the chewed piles and deposit them in the trash, and no one would be the wiser.

That worked for quite a while, but like all plans devised to deceive, eventually I was found out. One night after dinner, I couldn't wait to use the bathroom so I quickly went and rushed back just in time to see my sister pick up my plate and make the discovery, followed by an announcement. Funny what kids will do when they don't like their food!

How true that is in the case of God's kids, too. As we begin to chew on the meat of the Word, we discover something

112

we don't like. God says it's good for us. In fact, it may be the best part. But we've decided we don't like it, and it's something we can't swallow. So we pick and choose what we will tolerate, flushing this and that. It's not long before it becomes clear to those around us that we have created a god to suit ourselves. We have planned out, and determined what works for us. That's idolatry!

The truth is, we either believe what the Word of God says, or we don't. There is no picking and choosing what's good and what's not. It's all good, and we must feast on all of His word, to know His truths and will for our lives. It's a meal fit for a king and prepared by the King of all kings!

Psalm 34:8 Oh taste and see that the Lord is good; Blessed is the man who trusts In Him.

Lord,

Whet a passionate appetite in me for Your Word. May I delight in every morsel, as I study the scriptures. Your Word is alive and I want to know You more. Help me to taste and see that You are good, and to learn to trust You in everything, including the truth of Your word. In Jesus' name, AMEN

An Attitude of Gratitude

Ever felt as though God can't use you? Sometimes we feel so inadequate and we wonder how we could ever make a difference. I'm here to tell you that no matter what your circumstances are-God can use you!

I know this because I had the privilege of befriending one of God's most mighty prayer warriors. She wasn't famous, or on television, but her reward is grand. Her name was Mary and I did her hair every week in the care center.

She was a precious example to me of a willing servant for the Lord with an attitude of gratitude! She had lost both of her legs to amputation, and the rest of her body was so crippled with arthritis, that she couldn't feed herself or even scratch her nose. Her hands were all gnarled, and her body was so fragile that her bones would break just from the nurses trying to transfer her from the wheelchair into her bed. But she didn't let that get her down. She would lie in her bed and listen to praise and worship songs and pray for the employees at the care center, as well as the other residents, myself and my family.

She had only a small amount of money to her name left over each month after her expenses were paid. And with that money she would order little devotional booklets and have them distributed to many people throughout the care center. She would bring one to me and always include an extra for me to mail off to my son in the Navy.

Whenever I did her hair, many times she would prophesy and share scriptures with me and over the years there were times that she would ask if she could anoint me and pray for me. In her condition this was difficult to do, but she would instruct me to get a little bowl of water and put it under her curled up fingers and then place my hand under hers while she prayed for me. That wonderful woman of God prayed me through many hard circumstances of parenting four teenagers at once!

When it would be time for her to have a permanent wave, it was very difficult for her to sit that length of time, so we would pray the 3 weeks prior and while giving her the perm I would sing hymns to her to help pass the time. God was always faithful and she always made it through, with beautiful curls to boot!

We had an incredible friendship in the Lord. Each week as I would take her back to her room, she always had a piece of candy in her pocket that she had asked the nurse to place there. She'd look specifically for this little lady Eleanor, who had lost her ability to speak, and never had any visitors. Mary would always have me stop in front of Eleanor and hand her the piece of candy while she would say to her, "I love you and Jesus loves you too!" It would always cause Eleanor to tear up and reach out to touch Mary's arm for a brief moment. The exchange between those two was an eternal bond that brought us all to tears!

Mary was a prayer warrior of the greatest kind and she never accepted pity! I remember one day, another client had watched her come and go each week and approached her and touched her arm with compassion and said, "I feel so sorry for you." Mary just beamed back with a smile and sweetly said, "Why? I have Jesus!"

That's a picture of how we ought to live. With such an attitude of gratitude that no matter what comes our way we step up and not only try to make the most out of it, but actually make the BEST out of it! We ought to live with purpose, and live a life of excellence even though our circumstances may look hopeless. That's how Mary lived and I guarantee you-though she had no legs-her witness walked many miles in spreading the gospel of Jesus Christ. I have no doubt that she is dancing in heaven now!

Psalm 30:11-12 You have turned my mourning into dancing; You have put off my sackcloth and clothed me with gladness, To the end that my glory may sing praise to You and not be silent. O Lord my God, I will give thanks to You forever.

Father,

I praise You for the precious gift of Mary and the witness she was to all that knew her and those who heard of her faithfulness. Please Lord, may my attitude always be joyful even in affliction, knowing that You are my portion forever! Help me to preach the gospel to every creature for there is no higher form of gratitude that I could offer to You. Go before me now as I share Your message with a lost and dying world. In Jesus' name, AMEN.

Timing is Everything

You've heard it said that timing is everything? Well I'm here to tell you that's it's true! We are all called to share the Lord with those around us. None of us know how much time we have left. Therefore, we must be intent on sharing. However, this time I was so intent on sharing that I neglected to use wisdom in my timing!

My son was home on leave from the Navy, but preparing to ship out. It was shortly after the Sept. 11th tragedy that rocked our nation, and he would be headed to the gulf. I understood the danger. As we spent the day together, enjoying ourselves, the realization that I would have to tell him goodbye that day kept gnawing at the forefront of my mind.

When it came time for me to say goodbye, I sobbed, and hugged him ever so tight. I didn't want to let go. After all, who knew how long it would be before I would see him again. Or if I would see him again, for that matter?

As I headed down the street in my car, I suddenly realized that though I had told him I would be praying for him, I didn't actually pray with him, as I had planned. My son hadn't received Jesus as his Savior, and it was imperative I do this. I was already running late, but this was important. Yes, I would be taking this prayer into the very throne room of God myself, but I also knew this would be another opportunity to share with my son and plant another seed, and I just knew this was going to be the seed of all seeds!

I quickly turned the car around, pulled back in the driveway and breathlessly ran into the house. My son was nowhere in sight. His wife said that he was in the other "throne room" if you know what I mean?

"That's fine, I'll wait," I said. But as time went by, I grew desperate. I was going to be late and I had to leave-yet I wanted to pray. So I gently knocked on the bathroom door, and said," Son, I'm sorry. I realized that I didn't pray with you before I left, and I really wanted to".

He said, "That's okay, Mom."

I said," No, it's not okay. I want to lay hands on you, and pray for you before I leave."

He replied, "Mom, I'm going to the bathroom."

"That's all right, I'll wait, are you almost done?" I asked.

Now his tone grew more serious. "Mom, I'm going POOP!"

I didn't know what to do now. I knew his history, and knew this would take a long time, and I was already late, so in my thoughtless desperation I stammered, "Uh, okay, uh, that's okay, uh, You go ahead and keep doing that, and I'll stand out here and pray for you.

Now desperately pleaded, "MOM, PLEASE DON'T

STAND OUTSIDE THE DOOR AND PRAY WHILE I'M POOPING!"

It was then that I realized how ridiculous that sounded, and I had to chuckle. Yes, I'll admit it. I have the heart of a mother, who didn't think twice. I was desperate to share, but at that moment I think all I managed to do was scare my son. Just think, I could have scarred my child for life!

Sometimes we get so caught up in wanting to plant that seed that we forget about discernment as to timing and other factors crucial around us. Our hearts may be in the right place, but we lack wisdom. *The Bible says in Colossians 4:5-6 "Conduct yourselves with wisdom toward outsiders, making the most of the opportunity. Let your speech always be with grace, as though seasoned with salt, so that you will know how you should respond to each person.*

Maybe you're like me, and you think back of some of the crazy things you've done out of desperation to share Jesus. We've had zeal without knowledge. Don't let past failures keep you from sharing the good news of the gospel. Let's ask God to give us wisdom to be salt and light to this darkened world, in His perfect timing.

Lord, we admit we have failed at times in trying to share the good news of You with those we love. Forgive us for our ignorance. Grant us a greater wisdom as to when to share and what to share so that others run to You, instead of from You. Empower us to go boldly forward in proclaiming the truth of Your love, seasoned with salt, and bright enough for all to see. Prepare our hearts, and theirs, as You reveal the opportunities that You have set before us. Help us to make wise choices, through the grace and knowledge of You. In Jesus' name, Amen.

119

What's Happy All About Anyway?

I'm a mover! Have you ever heard anyone talk about be-ers and do-ers and the differences? Be-ers are the people who go through life real easy going,. They kind of saunter. They aren't in a hurry, and they are able to sit and just be! That's my husband. And then, there's the do-ers, always doing, needing to get things done. Sometimes so busy that they meet themselves coming and going. That's me! Let's just say-we help to balance each other out.

I have a hard time sitting. I'm a mover, and I attribute that to the fact that when I was growing up, we moved every year. By the time I was 16 years old we had moved 16 times, and my Dad wasn't in the military!

I was born in Illinois and my parents would buy old houses, then we'd move into them, fix them up, and just when they were perfect, sell them and start the whole process over again! There wasn't much time for sitting still. When I was 11, we moved to Arizona. My mom's health required it. She had lost her voice and hadn't been able to speak for 2 years. My 2 sisters and I thought it was great! She couldn't yell at us and we'd say "What? I can't hear you!" She would get frustrated, so she'd write it down and tap it with her finger several times. After moving to Arizona, however, she got her voice back within a week, and I'm actually glad, now, that she did.

My Dad was an alcoholic--not the happy kind, mind you. He could actually get quite mean, and add that to the fact that he had been in the Marines, and was a drill Sgt. wannabe complete with white glove inspections, made for a not so nurturing combo!

My Mom worked out of the home, so when it came to dealing with the everyday squabbles of 3 girls growing up, she didn't have the energy. Many times she'd say, "Don, handle it!" And he did!!!

Ever had your mouth washed out with soap? We got to choose our own little hotel size bar, hmmm, dial, ivory, or lava, which flavor? Here's a hint--don't choose the lava! We had to eat the whole bar while brushing our teeth with warm water at the same time--you know, to make lots of bubbles. I tease now and say that I ate so much soap as a child that sometimes I crave a couple of hotel bars and some salsa.

When I was 12, my parents divorced, and 2 years later, they re-married each other and divorced again when I was 21. That's a whole other story that didn't make the book, thankfully!

My parents had a rule that we couldn't date until we were 16 years old. I had no trouble adhering to this rule. Oh, did I mention I was a real looker??

Oh yeah, tall, very skinny, freckles, braces, and kidney bean shaped glasses, with a hairstyle like the Monkees. By now, you've probably gotten the visual. I want you to know, though, that I did update my look some. I let my hair grow, and got the wire rimmed stop sign shaped glasses. Oh yeah! I was cool!

When I was finally asked out, I fell in love with the first and only boy I ever dated. I think I felt as though no one would ever find me attractive. We were the same height when we started dating. I kept growing, but he didn't. I was barely 19 when we got married. I was 3 inches taller than he was which meant that he had to stand on blocks at our wedding for the pictures.

By the time I was 24 years old, I had given birth to 3 children, had 3 miscarriages, and my oldest child was 3 fi years old. I was UNHAPPY! My husband was a farmer, and a workaholic who worked 7 days a week, 12 hours a day. I was overtired, overwhelmed, and overburdened. I found myself crying a lot and wondering, "Is this all there is to life? Surely there's got to be more than this! This wasn't the life I had dreamed of!"

My love had dwindled away for my husband. I felt like I was raising these kids myself, so, why not do it on my own? I felt as though I had missed out on all there was to life. After all, everything I read and heard said that it was important that I was happy, and I wasn't. I became SELF absorbed, in the SELF movement that is so popular. I should do what makes me happy! I need to take care of my SELF first! I have a RIGHT to be happy, and I'm not.

So, at 26 years old, I separated from my husband and filed for divorce. My children were 5, 3, and turning 2. I was working out at the gym, and getting into great shape doing body building. Other men were finding me attractive. I was partying with my friends, drinking, and doing drugs, and living the life that goes with those things. Thankfully, the drugs were short-lived, because while smoking marijuana one night, I suddenly saw a bright light, only to later discover while looking in the mirror that I had actually set my bangs on fire! I kid you not--they looked like a tumble-weed on my forehead! I realized then--that I needed to stop!

In the meantime, while out one night, I met my current husband, Larry. I wasn't looking for a husband, but he was everything I wanted, AND he was taller than me!!! Now I had a boyfriend, and I had gotten a great job with UPS as a driver. I'll never forget that--I was so excited to get that job! I still remember when I got the call back. There were 2 spots open and 40 people up for the position, and I got one! The kids and I were holding hands, and dancing in a circle, singing "Mommy got the job! Mommy got the job!" They were so excited, and they had no idea why. At that time I remember proclaiming, "NOTHING can touch me now!"

I loved that job. It gave me a chance to stay in shape. I was muscular, had a great figure, made lots of money, had 3 wonderful kids, a terrific boyfriend, AND I had just purchased a brand new vehicle! I had it all-all the things I thought I needed to be happy!

Then one morning, I woke up with severe chest pain that radiated up through my jaw and down my arm. I was flat on my back and could barely breathe, with a heart rate of 120 beats per minute lying down. That's almost twice my normal rate. After several tests, I was diagnosed with "Acute Recurrent Pericarditis." That's an inflammation of the lining of your heart. Fluid builds up between your heart and the lining, and makes it difficult for the heart to beat and extremely painful to breathe.

Suddenly I couldn't work. I wasn't allowed to exercise. I was put on medications that caused me to gain a lot of weight AND deteriorated my bones. Each time I started to feel a little better, I would try to go back to work only to have it flare up again. I would have attacks, even when not working. I ended up having to sell my beautiful new vehicle, eventually give up my precious job, and absolutely NO exercising!! The things that I had taken so much pride in, that I thought I needed to bring me happiness were now stripped away. I felt worthless and anxious-the doctors were talking of open heart surgery or chemo medication. The side effects could be hair loss and boils on the face. I had already gained so much weight, and now, I would lose all my hair and get boils on my face?

I told the doctor, "Just kill me now!" How could Larry love me? I couldn't work. I wasn't looking like the woman he fell in love with. I felt very alone and fearful of what tomorrow might bring.

You know what ---God had a bigger plan! I had to stay home with my children, and as I did, I began to realize just how precious my children are. I started being the mom I should have been. Larry and I eventually got married, and we started living "respectable lives". We began attending a nearby church. I had gone to church as a child, off and on, and I knew that the Bible says that Jesus Christ is the Son of God, and that He died for our sins so that we could be forgiven, and He was buried in a tomb, and rose from the dead on the third day. I had been taught this in Sunday school, and now we felt it was time for the kids to be taught it also. In fact, I had asked Jesus into my heart when I was 12, at a church camp, but had long since forgotten that.

Years later, my Dad and step-mom, Katie, moved back to Arizona. They had been living in California, and now, Katie had a reoccurrence of her breast cancer. She sensed she wasn't going to make it this time and she wanted Dad close to his daughters--less than a half a mile away. They told me that now they had Jesus in their life, and that I needed Jesus too! Who were they to say anything? After all, what was the big deal? We were going to church.

Months passed and Katie's health continued to decline. In the last weeks of her life, I visited each day and I really grew to love her. I hadn't really known her before. Dying was something I had always been afraid of, and it wasn't easy watching her slip away. One day, my husband and I were both there visiting, and it had been about 3 weeks since she had been able to eat or drink anything. She was so weak. She asked me to have Larry come in and hold her up, because she wanted to sing me her favorite song. As she tried to clap, her hands were not matching up, and I couldn't make out the song she was trying to sing, so I called my dad in and he said, "Oh, she's singing, "Fear Not", and he began to sing, and clap," Fear not, for I am with you, fear not, for I am with you, fear not, for I am with you says the Lord."

As he was singing, her eyes were radiant with an expectancy of something joyful to come--I'll never forget it! She was dying, and her eyes held more hope than mine, and I was living --or so I thought. Each and everyday that she had left was precious, and each day I was seeing that her relationship with Jesus was real. It was more than attending a church--it was alive inside of her! In The Bible it says, "*If Christ is in you, though the body is dead because of sin, yet the spirit is alive because of righteousness.*"

After Katie's death, my Dad asked if we would all go to church with him. It would be his first time back to church without Katie. We agreed, and the people there were so friendly, they just seemed to glow! It was different from our church. They were clapping while singing, and we thought--Oh no! "Fanatics!!" I motioned to my family, "I know--let's just get through this." But, as we sang the songs, they really touched my heart.

As the weeks passed, I found myself revisiting Dad's church, on the weekends that Larry was gone fishing. I wanted to be there to support my Dad, and I started realizing I was missing something. I didn't quite understand, but I did know that the people there had it, and I wanted it!

What I was missing, was a RELATIONSHIP with Jesus. I had a RELIGION, but I didn't have a RELATIONSHIP!

Then the day came, when Larry was home, and we were getting ready for "our" church, but I had been feeling a very strong tug, and I told him that I felt as though we were to go to my Dad's church. This started a HUGE argument that ended with him leaving for our church without me! I kept watching out the window, thinking he would come back, but he didn't. I got ready, and went on to Dad's church. I was so saddened and confused. I was thinking, why would God want me to go to this church? I don't understand. I could lose my husband over this!

After singing, the Pastor prayed, and then gave us a special silent prayer time where I began pouring out my heart to God. I was crying, telling God I felt I was to come here, but why? I had messed up my life, and already had one failed marriage, but knew I wanted a relationship with Jesus, and I wanted Him to lead my life from then on. I loved my husband so much, but if I lost Larry because of this decision, to please give me the strength to get through it.

The Bible reminds me that "*I can do all things through Christ Who strengthens me!*" When I finished praying I opened my eyes, and Larry was sitting behind me.

From that moment on, I surrendered my life to Jesus Christ. He became FIRST in my life. My family was watching me and saw the difference. Jesus gave me the peace that I never had before, especially during difficult situations. I was content with my life, and with what I had. In fact, I was grateful. Jesus gave me true joy-deep within. I was no longer afraid of death. He saved my life. I had sinned against God, and His perfect standards, and I was headed for hell. But now, since I had turned from my sin, asked for forgiveness, and asked Jesus to lead my life from now on, I have the assurance I will go to heaven and live with Him forever! And I can't wait to see Him face to face!

That was Oct. 1994. Two years later, my husband trusted in Jesus as his Savior, and so did our daughters.

Since then, I have been healed from the "Acute Recurrent Pericarditis," and I can see now that God loved me so much that He put me flat on my back so that He could get my attention! And I am so grateful He did! I praise God for allowing circumstances that caused me to come to the end of myself, and recognize that no matter what I had, none of it mattered without Him. It could all be gone tomorrow. The Bible says, *"For what does it profit a man to gain the whole world and forfeit his soul"*

Remember when I thought it was all about me being happy? Happy is just an emotion, based on external circumstances. I now have the JOY of the Lord, and that's my strength! It's a joy that far surpasses happy any day!

I feel so blessed for this life of mine. God is in control! Has it all been a piece of cake since then? NO, but I will tell you that He has been there with me every step of the way, and He will never let go. He knows every detail of my situation. The Bible says this, "The Lord is my helper, I will not be afraid. What will man do to me? And God knows every detail of your situation too! Did you know that God so loved the world that He gave His one and only Son, that whoever believes in Him shall not perish but have everlasting life? It's true! Because God loves us so much, He sent His Son, Jesus, to die on a cross so that you and I could be forgiven of our sin and have eternal life. And He still would have done it--even if you were the only one! He loves you that much! That's His gift of grace, and it's free. We can't earn it. We must receive it by faith.

Every day He gives us is also a gift, and Katie used every precious last breath to share Jesus with me, and I've begun to ask myself, "What if this is my last day? How am I

127

using it?"

What about you, what if this is your last day? Remember when I said that I had sinned against God and His perfect standards? I had, and my sin was easy to see, but if you have ever told ONE lie, the Bible says that you have violated the 9th commandment. You have broken God's law and without Christ, you WILL face the wrath of God on Judgment Day! You see, God doesn't desire happiness, He requires righteousness, and that can only be achieved through Jesus Christ.

Jesus said, "I am the Way the Truth and the Life and no one comes to the Father, except through Me." We all will spend eternity somewhere - heaven or hell. Do you have the assurance that if this is your last day that you will go to heaven? You must repent, turn from your sin and turn towards God, ask for forgiveness, and put on the Lord Jesus Christ. Maybe you thought you received Him as your Savior a long time ago like I did, but never really understood, never repented, and fully surrendered your life to Christ and you want to do that now. Then, get right with God. Tell Him you're sorry. Pray something like this;

Dear Lord, Forgive me! I need you. I am desperate. I can't do it on my own anymore. I realize that I am nothing without You. Please forgive me of my sins, and change my heart. I want You to be Lord of my life, from this moment on. Thank you for dying on the cross and shedding Your blood for me. Give me the strength, help me to be strong, and from this day forward live only for You.

In Jesus' name I pray, AMEN.

Read your Bible everyday and obey what you read and God will never let you down!

ISBN 141203852-9

9 781412 038522